Claude J. Farley was born in Eveleth, Minnesota on December 29, 1935. He was educated at various colleges and universities in Washington, California and Washington, D.C. He received an M.A. degree in Religious Education from The Catholic University of America in Washington, D.C. in 1969. In 1967 he won the "Impact Teacher" award from the National Catholic Education Association for innovative teaching methods.

COVER PHOTO: *Tim Eagan*

"Be-Attitudes"

"BE-ATTITUDES"

AN INVOLVEMENT APPROACH TO TEACHING CHRISTIAN VALUES

Claude J. Farley

alba house

alba house

A DIVISION OF THE SOCIETY OF ST. PAUL
STATEN ISLAND, NEW YORK 10314

Current Printing (last digit):

9 8 7 6 5 4 3 2 1

Library of Congress Cataloging in Publication Data
Farley, Claude J
    "Be-attitudes"; an involvement approach to
teaching Christian values.

    1. Religious education of young people.
I. Title.
BV1485.F37   207'.12'79777   72-6753
    ISBN 0-8189-0260-4

Nihil Obstat:
    Edward Higgins, O.F.M.Cap.
    Censor Librorum
Imprimatur:
    †James P. Mahoney
    Vicar General, Archdiocese of New York
    June 17, 1972
The nihil obstat and imprimatur are official declarations
that a book or pamphlet is free of doctrinal or moral error.
No implication is contained therein that those who have
granted the nihil obstat and imprimatur agree with the
contents, opinions or statements expressed.

Designed, printed and bound in the U.S.A. by the Fathers
and Brothers of the Society of St. Paul as part of their
communications apostolate.

TABLE OF CONTENTS

INTRODUCTION

THIS BOOK BEGAN in my mind in the summer of 1966. I was walking on the streets of San Francisco and I saw a scene I would have captured if I had a camera, but it has been imprinted on my mind as indelibly as a photograph. I saw this: In the blistering sun of the afternoon the shadows began to deepen and to outline with striking clarity, the buildings of the city. I was impressed by one gigantic glass office building that stood as a monument to the modern world. And right in front of that building was an old, old church. The two buildings together made me think of the state of Christianity today. The Church in the city is old. It has a feeble voice. It is talking but the modern world is not listening. Then I thought again. It is not talking and the world is not listening.

Today, six years later, the Church seems to be finding its voice again. But it is a weak voice and the world is still not listening. All through the summer while I attended classes at the University of San Francisco my mind was racing with questions, answers, doubt, and confusion, but most of all with an underlying sense of excitement. I was studying under three of the modern world's great theologians: Fr. Bernard Haring, Fr. Barnabas Ahern, and Fr. Raymond Brown.

I had been teaching religion to teenagers for some time and their fresh approach to life, their creativity, their enthusiasm for their religion and world sparked in me the question: "Why not write a book that might be helpful to teenagers, parents and teachers of religion?" So that is what I decided to do.

I feel we need a fresh approach to the teaching and message of Jesus in the Gospels with regard to teaching teenagers—teaching teenagers the "really-reallies" of Christianity.

At the high school level we should be concerned primarily with the beatitudes—not with the beatitudes of the sixteenth century Council of Trent; not even with the beatitudes of the turn-of-the-century Council of Baltimore, which defines them as a listing of eight "Blesseds." Our concern should be to examine life in terms of "Be-attitudes," that is, our attitude toward "being," and specifically, toward "being Christian."

What are attitudes? Are they simply intellectual approaches to life-situations? Or are they more involved with the total person? Think about it for a moment. What do you do that is purely and totally intellectual, that is not connected somehow with the body, emotions or psyche? Yes, our attitudes encompass many of the complex mechanisms that make us human. They have tremendous influence on nearly every action of the day and night. Attitudes greatly influence our lives, and the way we live them.

Teenagers begin to make life-decisions in their teenage years, everything from choosing a career to marriage. Their attitudes toward being, their "Be-attitudes," will to a large extent determine those decisions.

One of my students wrote: "Maybe the youth of today loose their faith because they don't really understand Christianity. When their faith gets a jolt, it crumbles. Many think or at least they used to think, of Catholicism as abstinence from meat on Friday and attending Mass on Sunday. They don't realize one must be a Christian seven days a week, every day of the year."

By the time a student reaches seventeen or eighteen he doesn't want a religion of the past. He wants a religion of the *now*, and a religion of the future also. We know we have to get off the fence sometimes and make a commitment to Christ, and our job is to help the teenager prepare for his decision, "to be or not to be a Christian."

Our Lord said: "Would that you were hot or cold, but because you are lukewarm I begin to vomit you out of my mouth." Strong words, words that demand a strong decision.

"BE-ATTITUDES"

A human being is, in large measure, a mystery. A human being has the capacity to consciously control his decisions. Very little in our lives can be programmed like an IBM computer. We just don't live that way.

There are times in life to teach children, what Babin has called "privileged moments." These are the moments of grace when they can experience in a simple emotional way the presence of God. For example, I know a mother who teaches her children about the love of God by teaching them to love one another. For example, when the children come home from school the toddlers will run up to them, give them a big hug, and with sheer ecstatic joy say, "I love you!" The mother catches that moment of emotional love and joy to tell the children, "God loves you like that." What better way to teach about the love of God? In the course of this book, I will try to relate to you some of the "moments of humanness," moments of grace, privileged moments I have captured in teaching teenagers about the nature and purpose of Almighty God in creating this world and thinking so much of it as to send his only Son to redeem it.

So how do we teach teenagers about Christ? First, by letting him live in us. We can't give what we don't have. It's a fact that those who influence teenagers usually have a dynamic personality, a magnetic personality, an attractive personality. Sometimes, blinded by the flattery of it all, they let themselves become the end rather than the means.

We must, as teachers and parents, in our own individual lives, show teenagers that the very thing that attracts them to us is Jesus shining in our souls. It is so incredible, but we must believe it by an act of faith . . . that is the indwelling of the Holy Trinity.

I think we so often belittle adolescents for their sentimentality, their emotionalism, their giddiness, their irresponsibility, their schmaltzy taste. But we should build on it. For example, a typical teenager is just naturally spontaneous. Why not allow these teenagers to jump with sheer ecstatic joy as they jump and wiggle at their dances and games? Why not allow them to express themselves in the Liturgy in a way that is equally meaningful to them? Read the Psalms. See how often they remind us to be expressive.

> Alleluia!
> Praise God in his temple on earth,
> praise him in the temple in heaven,
> praise him for his mighty achievements,
> praise him for his transcendent greatness!
> Praise him with blasts of the trumpet,
> praise him with lyre and harp,
> praise him with drums and dancing,
> praise him with strings and reeds,

> praise him with clashing cymbals,
> praise him with clanging cymbals!
> Let everything that breathes praise Yahweh!
> Alleluia!

Ps 150

And again notice the spontaneity of man to God in Psalm 96.

> Sing Yahweh a new song!
> Sing to Yahweh, all the earth!
> Sing to Yahweh, bless his name.
>
> Proclaim his salvation day after day.
> Tell of his glory among the nations,
> Tell of his marvels to every people.
>
> Yahweh is great, loud must be his praise . . . .

Another important thing to remember about teenagers is their exceptional concern about love. Their music is filled with thoughts and expressions of love—puppy love, adolescent love and adult love. We as parents and teachers should capture this "privileged moment" in their lives and teach them about Christian love.

Christianity is all about love. Many of the youth of today don't really understand love, mainly because they have not felt it in their own lives. Their vision is fogged and they don't see the freshness and selflessness of real love. Maybe, too, the youth of our society do not mature fast enough. There is too much emphasis on fun, fun, fun and they do not mature enough to see the reality of what Christianity really is: "Giving of self to God and one's neighbor." In other words, "to love one's neighbor as oneself."

Teenagers are eager, if not ready, to take the leap of love, real love, the love of service. Notice the long waiting lists for work in the Peace Corps, PAV-LA, VISTA and related service organizations. And when these groups advertize they don't paint rosy pictures of what they will get out of their service. They tell it to the young person "as it is," and it's strictly to love other human beings because they are human beings. What are we doing to show the teenager that this is what Christianity is all about? How do we teach (poor word) love?

One more point of introduction: The concept of freedom. There is a drive and desire in every young person for freedom. I like to think of this freedom in the way St. Paul talks about it to the Galatians:

"When Christ freed us, he meant us to remain free."
Gal 5:1

And again, St. Paul says:

"My brothers, you were called, as you know, to liberty; but be careful, or this liberty will provide

XIII

> an opening for self-indulgence. Serve one another, rather, in works of love, since the whole of the Law is summarized in a single command: Love your neighbor as yourself. If you go snapping at each other and tearing each other to pieces, you had better watch or you will destroy the whole community."
>
> Gal 5:13-15

These words take some meditation. Freedom is not license and young people sometimes confuse the two. Young people clamor for freedom, and claim to be free. When they do this they don't like to admit a need, or a dependency on others. They come on strong sometimes, with an "I don't need God, or anyone else" attitude. This kind of attitude can be fatal for they need God most of all when they are in the process of becoming mature adults.

I think Christian youth, and especially Catholic youth, have it rough in today's society and Church. They are confused with the complexities of growing up in a complicated and swiftly changing society. But I also think that today's youth, *if* they work at becoming mature adults, work at knowing Jesus, and work at knowing themselves, can be the best Christians ever. This book will try to validate that statement.

This book is about attitudes. It is about the attitudes of Jesus Christ. This book is about the black and white city. It is about the mentally sound and the mentally retarded. It is about the bum on skid row. It is about the alcoholic writhing in bed and the thirteen-year-old kid who's had the scourge of divorce laid on his young back. It is about the old lady living in an old folks home, homeless with a roof over her head. It is about the Black thirsting for justice. It is about the prostitute crying for personal dignity. This book is about Jesus Christ and Christians who are trying to find the hungry, trying to give drink to the thirsty, trying to clothe the naked, trying to visit the imprisoned, and trying to shelter the homeless.

At Blanchet High School in Seattle, Washington, the Religion department introduced a new concept into the teaching of Christianity to teenagers. The basis, or guide line, for this course was taken from Matthew's Gospel, chapter 25:31-46, the last judgment scene. This in the final analysis, is the criterion against which one's Christian-Catholicism will be judged:

> When the Son of Man comes in his glory, escorted by all the angels, then he will take his seat on his throne of glory. All the nations will be assembled before him and he will separate men one from another as the shepherd separates sheep from goats. He will place the sheep on his right hand and the goats on his left. Then the King will say to those on his right hand, "Come, you whom my Father has blessed, take for your heritage the kingdom prepared for you since the foundation of the world. For I was hungry and you gave me food; I was thirsty and you gave me

drink; I was a stranger and you made me welcome; naked and you clothed me, sick and you visited me, in prison and you came to see me." Then the virtuous will say to him in reply, "Lord, when did we see you hungry and feed you; or thirsty and give you drink? When did we see you a stranger and make you welcome; naked and clothe you; sick or in prison and go to see you?" And the king will answer, "I tell you solemnly, in so far as you did this to one of the least of these brothers of mine, you did it to me." Next he will say to those on his left hand, "Go away from me, with your curse upon you, to the eternal fire prepared for the devil and his angels. For I was hungry and you never gave me food; I was thirsty and you never gave me anything to drink; I was a stranger and you never made me welcome, naked and you never clothed me, sick and in prison and you never visited me." Then it will be their turn to ask, "Lord, when did we see you hungry or thirsty, a stranger or naked, sick or in prison, and did not come to help?" Then he will answer, "I tell you solemnly in so far as you neglected to do this to one of the least of these, you neglected to do it to me." And they will go away to eternal punishment, and the virtuous to eternal life.

Mt 25:31-46

So, in class we began to ask ourselves, "Where are the hungry in Seattle? Where are the thirsty in Seattle? Where are the strangers in Seattle? Where are the naked in Seattle? Where are the imprisoned in Seattle?" The answers to these very important questions we tried to find by actually going out into

XVI

the city—searching, asking questions, discussing, interviewing, arguing, getting excited, being frustrated, etc. In short, our examination of what it means to be a Christian began to challenge us. We began to see that the easy questions and answers of the Catechism, when translated into everyday life by everyday people, could be very confusing, exciting, probing, discouraging and encouraging. It made us realize the emptiness of a faith not buttressed by deeds.

The actual structure within the classroom became somewhat difficult, bounded as we are by the four-walls-neat-rows-and-bells of school day existence. So we worked on the schedule and found that a revolving schedule, based on a four-day work week would provide us opportuntities to make our ideas operational. It works this way:

DAY ONE: On *Day One* we set up the question. For example, what is poverty? Who are the thirsty? Where are the homeless, etc. During the first day we might bring in a speaker who is an expert on the subject. Or we might show a film that touches the subject. Or I might lecture from my notes, and open the class up for discussion.

DAY TWO: On *Day Two* we would go into the city during the class period (preferably at the last period of the day to allow for additional time). The places we chose to visit I either preselected, or the students (on Day One) would select. For example, to learn about poverty we went to skid row, and the St. Vincent de Paul salvage depot. Then, to show contrast, we drove to the wealthy section of the city to "observe." During this time the students took notes and kept their eyes dancing for details.

At the beginning of this course I always tell my students of a story I once read, to illustrate awareness of the world around us. It goes something like this:

An old veteran newspaper editor sent a cub reporter out on an assignment to write a story about what takes place in a small grocery store. The cub reporter went out, a little bewildered at the assignment, and sat in a grocery store all day long. When he went home that night he wrote a story on what he saw. The next day, he submitted his story to the editor. What the editor read was the dry recounting of how many people came in and bought bread and milk and meat. How the owner of the grocery store rang up the money in the till. How he put the groceries in the sacks, etc.

After the editor read it, he threw it in the waste basket and turned to the reporter and said: "You didn't see anything! You didn't see the scratches on the glass counter made by the dimes and nickels. You didn't see the scuff marks on the door where people held the door with their shoe as they stumbled out with the groceries. You didn't mention the color of the sacks, or the bell in the till. You didn't see the fingerprints of children on the candy counter. You didn't see the wear on the counter where the grocer had countless times scraped the change into the palm of his hand. Boy, you didn't see anything. Life is made up of countless details that people miss, and because they miss the detail they don't see life! If you want to write about life, get out and see the details of life!"

I tell the students, "If you want to experience Christianity, and Christian living, see the details of life; see all of God's creatures and God's creatures' creations. I tell them to look for the circles under the eyes of the homeless; the dirt under the fingernails of the poor; to look beyond the windows of the homes of the poor and see the stuffing coming out of the mattresses. I feel if they can become aware of the details of life in their vibrant teenage years, they will become more-aware-Christians in their adult life.

So, on *Day Two*, we don't just ride into the city, we view it under a microscope!

DAY THREE: On *Day Three*, back in the classroom, the students either form a large circle (the entire class), or several smaller ones and begin to discuss what they had seen, heard, experienced, emotionally felt, what they thought about and questioned.

The results of this are staggering. Fresh, alert teenagers can see the now-world through new eyes, and the view is exciting. One seventeen-year-old wrote:

"I never thought of the alcoholic as thirsting for personal worth. Maybe that's what Christ had in mind when he said: 'Give drink to the thirsty!' 'Drink' can be spiritual as well as physical. How interesting."

DAY FOUR: On *Day Four* the discussion resumes where it left off on Day Three. Only at this point do the students begin to ask new questions and arrive at new answers. They discuss and argue and project new ideas and try to come to some tentative conclusions.

As a teacher, I do not expect these sessions to permanently form the students' ideas about Christ and Christianity. I feel, though, that these experiences are preparatory for that unknown time in their lives when they do decide to live a fully committed Christian life.

CONCLUSIONS: In order to make the students concretize their own ideas, I have them write out on paper (to be handed in), their personal reactions to, experiences with, thoughts about or feelings toward Christ and Christians in Seattle.

The burden of this book will be to try to share with you, the reader, this new and exciting age of Christ as seen through the eyes of teenagers, and some adults, in a very real, modern world.

The Poor

"... in your lifetime, Dives, you had good things, but Lazarus was poor."

CHRISTIANITY CAN'T be taught. It must be experienced. So how about poverty? Does one have to be poor to be a Christian? Christ loved the poor. He went out of his way to be with the poor. He identified himself with the poor. He recommended evangelical poverty to a select few of his closest followers.

Where are the poor in your city? *Who* are the poor is perhaps a better question.

In our class we tried to find the poor by going out into the city of Seattle. We found them. These teenagers bouncing with vitality and glowing without "Lady Clairol," saw people with stringy hair and circles under their eyes. They saw people with dirt under their fingernails—dirt that hadn't been absent for years.

"BE-ATTITUDES"

We had gone to the local St. Vincent de Paul salvage bureau where the so-called "bums" look for a hand-out but have to work for it. Here discarded dolls are redone by deaf-mute women while men with handicaps of all kinds, rejected by other employers, do insignificant jobs sweeping the sidewalks and fixing tricycles. The place has the smell of a fumagator which "de-lices" old sofas and chairs. It's cold in the winter and hot in the summer. But it's "someplace" for many poor people.

The students walked around this place with wide-eyes. One girl said in her paper:

> "As Christians we are obligated to help in some way. As I walked through St. Vincent de Paul I thought: 'Oh, Lord, I'd die if I had to wear clothes like this.' It was almost terrifying to think that some people really have to. I hope that someday *all* people will care enough about their brothers, black or white, not to let them suffer like these people must do."

Another girl said:

> "I don't know what poverty is. Poverty is still undefined for me. When we went down to the St. Vincent de Paul Bureau I could hardly say I saw poverty."

Another said:

> "This is what I saw:

2

Dirty children
holes in pant knees ...
Dirty parents
hunting through garbage ...
Kindness.
Drunkenness.
Misery.
Cigarettes hanging from mothers' mouths.
Lack of discipline.
Lack of love.
Achievement.
Abuse.
Fighting. Playing.
Many poor, many wealthy.
Despair.
Want.
Wonder.
Christ!"

We also walked through the poorer section of town, very briefly. A *brief* visit is sufficient to have the kids catch on. I quote from one of their papers:

"I felt all during the time I was observing, that Christianity was present in organizations and institutions, but going down First Avenue was so enlightening! The train station was full of men who had no family. No home to 'go home to.' No one to love them. They looked so forlorn and miserable.

"But what could I do to help them? It actually hurt just to walk by and not do something to relieve their misery. It's frustrating. I suppose many people like me

3

see them everyday, and walk by. They probably don't even give a second thought to them. I saw three old men walk up to the garbage can, open the lid and plow through it looking for anything usable. How wasteful we are! How fortunate! Too fortunate! Too wasteful! 'Blessed are the poor in Spirit, for theirs is the Kingdom of Heaven.'"

I tell the students of Jesus' explanation of what our attitude should be toward poverty. He has many, but I use the story of the rich man and Lazarus.

"There was once a rich man who dressed in the most expensive clothes and lived in great luxury every day. There was also a poor man, named Lazarus, full of sores, who used to be brought to the rich man's door, hoping to fill himself with the bits of food that fell from the rich man's table. Even the dogs would come and lick his sores. The poor man died and was carried by the angels to Abraham's side, at the feast in heaven; the rich man died and was buried. He was in great pain in Hades; and he looked up and saw Abraham, far away, with Lazarus at his side. So he called out, 'Father Abraham! Take pity on me, and send Lazarus to dip his finger in some water and cool off my tongue, for I am in great pain in this fire.' But Abraham said, 'Remember my son, that in your lifetime you were given all the good things, while Lazarus got all the bad things; but now he is enjoying it here, while you are in pain....'" Lk 16:19-25

The story goes on to say how Lazarus could not reach over the gulf that separates them, nor could he

4

help the rich man's brothers who already had what he had on earth. This is a very subtle story. Jesus was very clever. He did not condemn poverty. He did not condemn riches. He merely pointed out that the reason the rich man went to hell was because "he didn't *see* Lazarus." Notice, the rich man did not persecute Lazarus, telling him to get off his steps. Nor did he send his servants to dispose of Lazarus. The rich man simply *did not see* the poor man Lazarus. I think that we, as teachers, must show our students where and what poverty is. We should exhibit in our lives a concern and compassion for the poor. Then, and only then, will they begin to see the connection between Christian living and poverty.

It was a moving experience for my students to go down to "where the poor are," and *see* people who are materially poor. Now, for the first time, they began to realize that real people suffer from lack of food and clothing. Jesus said to take care of the poor. Now, at least they knew where they were. Someday, perhaps, they will be in a position to do something about it.

Another project we undertook was to send a tape recording to a Deputy Administrator in the Office of Economic Opportunity in Washington, D.C. The students asked questions about the poor, and what the United States Government was doing about them, etc.

5

"BE-ATTITUDES"

The man from the O.E.O. was most gracious and sent back a tape listing some statistics about the "official" view of poverty. He said that anyone who makes less than $3,000.00 per year is considered by the United States Government as "poor." He went on to say that out of 47 million familes, 9.3 million earn less than $3.000 annually. Five million live in cities and 4.3 million live in the South. Six million have a family head with less than a ninth grade education. Two million are non-white, 2.3 million have a woman as the family head, 3.2 million have a family head 65 years or older.

These are statistics. They do not touch young people's lives. They must somehow experience it, discuss it, feel it, smell it, handle it, taste it.

To try to do this in another way we made another tape recording and sent it to Harlem. Seattle, psychologically speaking, is about as far from Harlem as the moon. Our notions of Harlem were "newspaper" notions and "movie" notions. Ideas we gleaned second hand.

We addressed ourselves to students in Rice High School in the heart of Harlem. We asked these students what evidence of poverty they had seen. The tape we made lasted for about ten minutes and as we played it back to ourselves, we heard ourselves saying, though we didn't say so in so many words. "We white, middle-class, secure, Catholic teenagers in Se-

6

attle want to know what you black, poverty-stricken teenagers in Harlem feel like being poor." An insult? We saw it, but didn't intend it to be so. That was us, and we wanted to be honest and open in seeking the truth. We expected to get hurt mentally and spiritually in the exchange. This is what happened:

The students' eyes began to glow like saucers when they played the tape from the boys in Harlem. They were simply extraordinary in their humility and kindness toward us. One of the Harlem kids said:

> "Dear fellow students. I've lived in East Harlem all my life and I can say that I have seen just about everything there is to see. I appreciated very much hearing from your tape, but I got the impression from your opinions that you thought Harlem is totally poverty-stricken.
>
> "Yes, there is poverty, prostitution, alcoholism, crime and delinquency in this city, but with so many people that live in this city by proportion there should be more of anything here than in most cities."

When asked if he had ever seen poverty, he said:

> "Yes, I have seen poverty. I live in perhaps the worst block in New York City, according to *The New York Times*. The street? It stinks. There is all kinds of drugs in the streets. There is a friend of mine who lives down the block. I think he's poor. He doesn't have a father, and his mother is always gone. So I bring him

7

to my home so that he won't feel bad. I try to joke with him and cheer him up."

As we sat in our clean classroom, a whole nation away, we were stunned! He said it in such a simple, humble way. No fanfare, no bitterness, no deceit. He said it: "Love your neighbor as yourself." I've never heard it said the way he did: "I bring him to my home so that he won't feel bad. I try to joke with him and cheer him up." Charity comes in many forms. This is one of the purest.

This same young man was asked on the tape by his teacher if he had ever seen rats in his apartment house. He answered:

> "Oh, yes, in my old apartment I did, but then we moved from that place. We used to see rats all the time. My brothers and sisters and I used to throw our shoes at them as they came out from underneath the refrigerator."

Asked if he had ever known anyone who was bitten by a rat, he said:

> "Yes. I was once. I was sitting on the side of my bed putting on my shoes in the morning and this big rat came and 'slapped' me on the side of the foot. It was a terrifying experience."

"It was a terrifying experience...." This has been emblazoned on my mind like a firebrand. This young

8

man has to suffer because he lacks. I am materially comfortable. Why? Statistics, like the dry bones in the Valley that Ezekiel describes, begin to be clothed with flesh and blood when they are spoken by a real teenager, in a real world of poverty.

I asked the girls in my class if they would like to experience a kind of "poverty" for one week. I asked them to give up make-up for one week and to try to live on one dollar for a seven-day period, as many poor kids do. Reaction? Nobody did it. One girl, in writing her reaction to this whole unit on poverty, said very honestly:

> "I know now what Christ meant when he said to take care of the poor. I am so selfish with all that I have—my family, my nice home, my clothes. I couldn't even bear to live one week with no make-up. May God give me the courage to live a Christian life for which apparently I am not yet ready."

We cannot, as Christians, be content with paying our taxes and letting the United States Government take care of the nation's poor. Jesus never did this. He went out to them. He became involved with them. So much so, that the vast majority of people did not recognize him: "Who is this man? Isn't he from Nazareth? Isn't he the carpenter's son?" "He eats with sinners...."

9

"BE-ATTITUDES"

Teenagers today are worldly-wise, more so than adults give them credit for. One of the students said this:

> "My parents feel that the only solution to the poverty problem is to give the poor money. They feel that it is not worth it to train the people for jobs because this has not worked in the past. They feel that a guaranteed annual income would solve the poverty problem, and that the rest of the people should pay taxes, so the money can be given to the poor.
> "I disagree with this because I think that giving them money will only gloss over the problem. It won't solve anything. These people won't know how to use money, and they will never realize the true value of money. I think these people should be trained, and jobs created for them so that they can feel a sense of accomplishment in themselves."

Another said:

> As Christians, we have to be what Christ said and help them get out of their poverty. If we don't help, or don't even care, then we are not really Christians. We have to learn to love these people for what they are and for what they must be going through. One must realize that most poor people are not poor because they want to be, or because they are lazy. We even have to help the lazy because they deserve a good life just as much as anyone else, even if they are lazy. I know most people would be if they had nothing to look forward to in life. Most poor people are born

10

in poverty and there is not much they can do. They need the help of others.

"I think that if we keep ignoring the problem it will continue to get worse and many people will never see the goodness in the world just because of our ignorance."

Teenagers are optimistic about their world, and I think we should encourage that optimism. If they are optimistic about erradicating poverty, we, as adults, should back them. Perhaps they will come up with new and better ideas to do this. So be it. Let's listen to them. They have a new hold on Christianity that we perhaps did not have in our day and age and we should not frustrate their role in the cause of Christ.

The Homeless

WHY A *Christian* TEENAGER? Because, in their process of growth to that Christian commitment, the Christian teenagers must *experience* what Jesus said and did. He said, "I was a stranger, hungry, sick, and without shelter and you made me welcome." (Mt 25)

Jesus himself "had nowhere to lay his head." He said, "When you did it for the least of my brothers, you did it for me."

In order to "experience" homelessness we did two things. First, the director of Catholic Charities in the Archdiocese of Seattle came and talked to the class on Day One. His opening sentence was: "There are no more orphans in the United States, but there are plenty of homeless people. All the orphans, illegitimate kids, etc., are taken care of by the State. Very rarely do you find babies left in blankets on door steps. They are born in sterilized hospitals, then whisked away to be taken care of by the State."

"However," he went on to say, "there are many homeless kids—teenagers, below and above. The home is where the heart is, and for many, many people there is no heart, no love, no home."

He went on to say that two-thirds of the State's budget is given to welfare. That isn't much if you say it fast, but millions of dollars each year go to the care of homeless children and adults. How many hearts in that?

Second, one nippy October morning my class and I got into our cars and drove down to skid row to find the homeless. We found them.

We had previously defined "the homeless" as a person who had no love, security or warmth to share with another. Homelessness doesn't mean the absence of four walls and a roof.

On Seattle's First Avenue, there is a Jewish pawn broker. He makes a living at selling old typewriters, dusty lamps, flashy circus clocks, knives and guns. But besides the business, Ruby gives of himself to the "derelicts," the "unfortunates" of skid row. He helps the prostitutes, drug addicts, drunks, alcoholics, ex-cons and teenagers who land there because it's the only place they are accepted. This is *how* he helps.

He welcomes them to his pawn shop. He sits on a little stool behind the counter and they sit or stand in front of the counter or behind. Behind him is a

General Electric coffee urn that has a constant supply of coffee. The sight of it, and the ever present half-full glass cups would make the Health Department shiver. But there's more than coffee there, more than a place to sit. Ruby's Pawn Shop is a "home" for people who have no place to go. Ruby's Pawn Shop is a welcome for people whom *nobody* welcomes.

Let me give you an example of how this man offers the welcome Christ would offer if he were there. While my students and I were standing in the two-by-four shop listening to Ruby, in came a young girl about twenty. We'll call her Judy, pushing a baby buggy with a beautiful little boy who had Negro features.

Judy was obviously pregnant. She was skinny except for her bulging belly. She had spaghetti black hair, and three teeth missing from her lower left jaw. She wasn't ugly, she was dirty.

Behind her came a bean pole of a man, about twenty too. He was pale and emaciated, Judy's "husband." When Ruby saw them come in he waved and said, "Come on in! Judy come here. Skinny (the husband) you too. Want you to meet Mr. Farley and some of his students from Blanchet High." So they inched their way through the group of kids, with shiny Lady Clairol hair. Ruby then asked for the baby. He picked him up beaming and the baby smiled back. The usual baby talk and girls cooing over the

15

cute child took place—then a curious thing happened. Judy went over quietly and sat down and put her head on her forearm. It was five minutes before Ruby noticed her. When he did, he went over to her and put his arm over her shoulder and asked her how she felt. She didn't feel good she told him. In fact she wanted to throw up. So he helped her to her feet, and back to a "bathroom" he had at the rear of the shop.

Out front we went on talking and I drifted back to see if I could help. Just as I got to the back Ruby came storming out, swore and said to me, "She hasn't had anything to eat! Damn it!" He roared out and yelled at Skinny, "How come you didn't see to it she didn't get some food in her stomach today?" "She had breakfast," he said. "No she hasn't, stupid. She's trying to throw up and she can't. She's hungry. Go out and buy her something." And with that he gave him a dollar to get some food. Shortly, Skinny came back with a hamburger and a milk shake for his pregnant, sick wife. He gave the hamburger to her and she devoured it like a vacuum cleaner.

All during this scene, cut from the raw fabric of human life, the students stared with big eyes, and ears wide open. And when Judy, the baby and Skinny left, Ruby said, "She's a prostitute. He's a pimp. She had the first baby by another guy, and God knows who's the father of the baby she is now carrying. She's never had any love in her life. Her mother abandoned her as a child and she is crying out for love." Then he began to teach the students. He said something like: "You kids are well scrubbed, and have nice houses and cars and parents and teachers who care about you. Be grateful for all you have. And another thing—don't condemn them people here on the Avenue. They're not bad. They have no pride in themselves. No one gives a damn about them."

Through all of this the students didn't say much . . . but believe me they were listening.

Then in came an old man on crutches. He had on an old dirty grey top coat, two sizes too large for him. If you wet your finger and ran it down the side of his face you'd leave a white mark. When he opened the door, Ruby smiled and told him to "come on in and have a cup of coffee." He shuffled through the kids and sat down. He was surrounded by the teenagers and Ruby introduced him to us. He simply smiled.

Our conversation went on and the old man didn't say a single word, but we could tell that he was thrilled to be able to sit in a group of kids and be accepted.

This is a simple true-life story. It really happened. There were others in the pawn shop—Ruby's friends. There was an ex-con—a handsome, strong, tough-look-

17

ing young man. There was a twenty-year-old who looked forty. Ruby asked him to tell the students his story. He did. He was on heroin, trying to kick the habit started by his father—and so on and on.

From the outside these people are bums, good-for-nothings—they are "peculiar" people to put it charitably. Simon and Garfunkle in their song, *A Most Peculiar Man* tell the story of a man about whom nobody cared, who was alone—the same man we saw in Skinny and Judy, the baby, the ex-con, the drug addict and the old man, people who lived in flop houses because they had no home.

The students' reaction to this new world was eye-opening:

> "To me, the visit to the pawn shop was really enlightening. I'd always heard about people like Judy and the drug addict, but I always thought of them as being some place else and not here in our own city. I always thought, 'It could never happen here,' but who was I trying to kid?"

> "When we were down there, I got the strong urge to do something right then and there to help them, but then we left in our nice cars and came back to our nice school and nice houses, and the reality of the people down on the 'Avenue' became just a memory."

> "I really admire Ruby for what he is doing. Those people need to be accepted, wanted and loved and he

is doing just that. I know we as Christians should be doing something too, but I don't know what. Most of us are too afraid to leave the warmth and security of our little worlds."

Yes, this teenager didn't know what to do, but she saw for the first time what it means to be a Christian, to be concerned about other persons as they are—not as we would want them to be, but *as they are.* If she is allowed to think about her world with the freedom of Christ; if she is allowed to continue to be aware of her now-world, she'll find some of the answers . . . and she'll do something about the problems. Teenagers can't be expected to know "what to do." The world is dawning on them, for the first time in many cases, and they have to have the freedom to discover it and, in the process, they will find themselves.

Another said:

"As I watched Judy and the two boys talk I could tell how inferior they felt and how much they really do want to be accepted in society. The problem is that they need help—and a great deal of it. This help can come from young Catholic adults, such as ourselves."

"If the older generation only realized what being a Christian really means they would probably help too,

19

but they don't; therefore the responsibility lies with us and I sometimes wonder if we can handle it."

"While we go on leading our nice sheltered, love-filled lives what will happen to the homeless on the Avenue?"

Home is being loved, cared for, understood and appreciated for being what you are, not what your parents or others wish you could be. In other words home is being accepted by your family. Home is security. Home is having someone to confide in and tell your problems to.

Christianity is a group of Christians who are trying to spread Christ's rule or pattern for living to others. It is loving your neighbor, whether friend or enemy, as yourself and living up to this!

When we visited skid row that eighteen-year-old boy seemed to know he was heading for trouble, but he did not seem to be concerned about it, just as if he were not going to try and prevent himself from slipping into it.

After we left the pawn shop and threaded our way through the traffic of the city the students began to talk. They were angry, frustrated, overwhelmed by what they saw, dumbstruck, questioning. One eighteen-year-old said,

"There's what Christ meant! That's it! That's what it means to be a Christian! Not simply going to Mass on

Sunday, wearing nice clothes that others will see and admire—and be envious. That's right. Too many adults think that to be a Catholic all you have to do is go to Mass on Sunday and go to Confession once in a while."

What it really takes to be a good Catholic is to be Christian seven days a week.

The Ghettoed

THE RACIAL PROBLEM is supposed to have started when Cain killed his brother, Abel. All kinds of myths have conveniently grown up to satisfy mainly the whites that Cain's "mark" was the blackening of his skin by the sun to show God's displeasure with him. Hence, all black people are supposed to be on God's "Black List" and anyone who is not feels somewhat superior.

Racial problems are problems of attitude.

Black is Bad
Yellow is Coward
Red is Hate
Brown is Quiet
White is Pure
Grey is the Mind
Of the man who
Can't

"BE-ATTITUDES"

> See
> Past colors
>   to
>   Himself!
>   (*Kathy Farrow*)

It would be the understatement of the century to say that in our American society today there is a racial problem. For too long black ghettos have been rotting like garbage in the dumps of the city's slums. So long, in fact, that when one thinks of slums he generally thinks black.

Some of the questions this generation asks is: "Why did the black people allow it? Where were the Christians?"

Another question a Catholic must ask himself is: "Where was the Church, where was I, when so many people were hurting so badly? Didn't Jesus *explicitly* deal with this problem of man's inhumanity to man?" Yes, he did. Here it is:

> There was a lawyer who, to disconcert him, stood up and said to him, "Master what must I do to inherit eternal life?" He said to him, "What is written in the Law? What do you read there?" He replied, "You must love the Lord your God with all your heart, with all your soul, with all your strength, and with all your mind, and your neighbor as yourself." "You have answered right," said Jesus, "Do this and life is yours." But he, wishing to justify himself, said to Jesus, "And who is my neighbor?"

24

Jesus answered, "A certain man was going down from Jerusalem to Jericho, and he fell in with robbers, who after both stripping him and beating him went their way, leaving him half-dead. But, as it happened, a certain priest was going down the same way, and when he saw him he passed by. And likewise a Levite also, when he was near the place and saw him, passed by. But a certain Samaritan as he journeyed came upon him, and seeing him, was moved with compassion. And he went up to him and bound up his wounds pouring on oil and wine. And setting him on his own beast, he brought him to an inn and took care of him. And the next day he took out two denarii and gave them to the inn-keeper and said, "Take care of him; and whatever more you spend, I, on my way back, will repay you."

"Which of these three, in your opinion, proved himself neighbor to him who fell among the robbers?" And he said, "He who took pity on him." And Jesus said to him, "Go and do you also in like manner."

(Lk 10:25-37)

Why did it take a decision of the Supreme Court of the United States in 1954 which prohibited segregation in U.S. schools, to wake us up to the fact of unchristian injustices in our Christian nation? Where did all the Christians go?

These are questions, not accusations, but it would be an interesting Ph.D. study in Psychology—to find out why Christians have not been as concerned about their brothers as they ought to have been in the past,

25

to find out why more of the clergy were not shouting from the housetops against so obvious a breach of Christian charity. I think Jesus would have. I think he would have stood on street corners, before microphones, in front of TV cameras and shouted till the blood veins stood out on his neck, and his face grew crimson, shouting to Christians to *love!*

But how in the world does one "teach" love of neighbor? Because that's what it boils down to—a teacher in a classroom is expected to "teach" Christian charity. A mother or father at home is expected to "teach" love of neighbor—this is basically Christian. If a home or school doesn't have this it simply isn't Christian. How do you do it? Well, there's a way not-to-do-it. I remember seeing a film called *Willie Catches On,* a story of how prejudice is taught in very subtle, and really, non-conscious ways by parents. For example, telling a child after he has come in from play, "You're as black as a little nigger! Go in and wash up!" Or using the noun "Jew" as a verb, meaning to cheat someone out of something. Attitudes are picked up by children like dust in a vacuum cleaner! So how do you verbally teach Christian attitudes? You don't. An attitude is a way of life. It can only be absorbed. That's why good example is so important. It's as simple as that.

When I faced this opportunity in the classroom I didn't quite know what to do. I asked myself, "How do you teach these seventeen and eighteen-year-olds that to be a Christian one must *love* his neighbor as Christ did and taught us to? I thought I did, but I lived in a white ghetto all my life. I went to all white schools, and I remember peering out through my white eyes as a boy, and wondering if the Negro body was *all* black. My formal education—high school, college and theology—was all in white schools. I found myself saying: "What do *you* know about the problem today? You're no expert—could you even begin to teach this?"

So I did the next best thing. I brought in black people to talk to my students. We went as a class to the Central area to talk to them in their homes or Community Centers. We saw films and watched videotapes dealing with black and white people living as black and white with a lot of grey mixed in.

One year the students and I arranged with another school that was mixed to have home visits. We went to their homes and talked about the problem of black and white and where the Christian fits into the picture. When I mentioned this to a few adults they thought it was a good idea, but wondered if it was "practical." "Didn't *they* think you were coming down to watch them?" "What did the parents think?" "Did the teenagers talk?" Yes, the teenagers talked—and talked with a frankness and openness that was refreshing. There's great hope for racial

27

understanding in this country if we let the young people handle the situation.

One of the most powerful television documentaries I ever saw was called *Time for Burning*—the actual life drawn of a Lutheran Parish in Omaha, Nebraska. Briefly, a group of teenagers under the direction of the Pastor (Youngdahl) got together to talk about their racial problems. I remember one thing one of the black kids said after another had condemned the Churches for not doing something about the racial injustice in the United States. She said, "It's not the Church's fault. It's the peoples'! People make up the Church!" And that's it exactly. People make up the Church and it's high time we stop thinking of "the Church" as the scapegoat for everything from racial injustice to war. Christians, individual Christians, must be aware of what it means to be a Christian and then begin to live like one.

In the Lutheran Parish in Omaha, the teenagers suggested that the adult couples get together and talk. To be very conservative and cautious they suggested that ten black couples visit the ten white couples just to talk. Well, there was such a furor over the suggestion that Pastor Youngdahl found himself in the middle of a violent racial storm. Some of his parishioners said it wouldn't hurt anything to talk . . . at least talk. But others, and as it turned out, the majority, were against integration of any kind. In fact, they were so adamant that they sought, and got,

Pastor Youngdahl's resignation. Jesus said: "Love one another as I have loved you." "Love the Lord your God with your whole mind, will, strength and soul; and love your neighbor as yourself."

To bring it closer to home, I asked my students to write a paper after spending some time examining the racial problem. This is what one wrote:

"First of all, I would just like to say that I don't know if my attitude can be classified as Christian or non-Christian. For anyone to say they are better than anyone else is wrong. All men are equal.

"I didn't realize just how prejudiced people can be until my sister and I had a discussion with some older people one night. My parents were there and I was really in for a big surprise. Oh, sure, they say equal opportunity for Negroes and all, but they sure don't believe it, or really practice it. They would no more associate with Negroes personally then they would let us date a Negro. I am sure if a Negro family moved in near us they would have some fine comments to make about 'those' people!

"Finally, the discussion ended with my father making the remark, 'Is that what *they* teach you at *that* school? Is that what we're paying good money for?'"

(I've never had such a compliment as a teacher!)

She continues... "I was shocked to say the least! I know that when I see a Negro or any other person who is different than myself, I don't see his color, I see

29

the person for what he or she is. Isn't that how you should see all God's children?

"I don't think I'm wrong to want Negroes for my friends. I know some of my very best friends are Negroes. But is that anything extraordinary? It shouldn't be.

"And as for dating Negroes, all I can say is that it depends on both individuals involved. I know myself, I am particular as to whom I go out with. I think the same thing applies with mixed-race dating. I won't go out with a person just because he's a Negro. He must have what I am looking for in a person."

And that's the crux of the question. What's the individual person's attitude toward another individual? The "Be-attitudes" of living. The "Be-attitudes" toward another person's being!

Here's what one cynically perceptive young lady wrote:

"Joe Brown is a Negro. He lives in the Central Area in an old dilapidated house. He doesn't give a hang about his house, but he has a huge color television and a brand new shiny pink Cadillac. He's paying for it on the easy installment plan.

"Joe goes to dances every Saturday night and he's the sharpest cat on the floor. After the dance Joe goes to the nearest tavern, gets smashed, and then staggers home to beat up his wife and fifteen kids. Things just get him down.

"Joe can't get a job, so his wife washes clothes and moonlights as a prostitute. Maybe that's why he has so many kids . . . .

"Anyone can see from the unbiased, non-prejudiced report that all niggers live like animals and will never be worth nothing. We whites know, that's all. Some day they'll learn how to live respectably like we do."

Young people today see hypocrisy in many of their elders and they don't like it. They lash out against it, some violently. Let us hope that the next two generations will be much more understanding and open toward each other than the present two seem to be.

I feel that the current generation of teenagers can become the best Christians ever if they don't drop the ball. If they can be helped to see what is involved in being a Christian, with their hope, love and enthusiasm, they will truly be zealous to open up this world for Christ. What a tremendous force for good that will be!

I asked the question: "The Negro and the Christian American: 'What's the problem?' " Here are a few reactions. Think about them.

"No one wants to give."

"The problem, I think is that white people don't think they are equal to blacks and they consider them lower. I think we are all equal because God made us to be the way we are. If he wanted us to be all the same color he would have."

31

"I think it's the prejudice of our parents and their generation. My parents, particularly my mother, would never let me go out with a Negro boy. She is even a bit peeved about my tutoring a Negro boy at the St. Peter Claver Center. Surely we are old enough to make our own decisions, but as long as we live with our parents we can't do anything about it."

That may be a glib excuse, blaming parents for the problems of racial injustice, but if one could get inside the mind of a teenager and get him to really want to do something on his own—then we'll have progress in the next fifty years like we've never had before.

Some want to go slowly with the problem. "Don't rush it," they say, "we can't change the world overnight." Yet today cars go 80, 90, 100 mph. The movies are super. Television is in color. Clothes are mod ... so is the racial problem. Wonder why we can't go just as fast, and be as inventive with this problem too?

Life Magazine in its March 8, 1968 issue published a most brilliant piece of journalism. It dealt with the whole gamut of the Negro-racial problem in the United States. On the cover was the picture of a Negro boy crying his heart out in despair. The issue is well worth reading. In fact, a *must* if one is to understand the real racial problems of our day. It lets you get inside the skin of a Negro and look out through his eyes. And the view is much different.

Letters to the Editor in the following issue were very interesting:

> "Sirs: My twelve-year-old son read the story of the Fontenelle family and was heartsick. His question was, 'What can we do to help them?' I feel helpless. How can I answer my child's question?"

And another:

> "Sirs: How many wept tears of frustration as I did? Where *does* one begin? How does one begin?"

A man named Gordon Parks wrote the story of the Fontenelle family and he made a comment in the subsequent issue. I thought it was very telling.

> "Like *Life*, I have received hundreds of letters and questions asking, 'What can I do?' The answer is far too big and complex for me to attempt: society must give its conclusions. I can only speak through personal experience.
>
> "If you wish to turn my anger—the Negro's anger—from you, acknowledge me and my needs.
>
> "I could rattle off a thousand incidents that feed my hostility. I seldom do because I feel that you live too deeply in a hard reasoning of your own. You have heard plenty about the ghetto houses, the rats and roaches, the need for bread and work. I'm talking about the casual little happenings you create for me that continuously nourish my anger and dismay.

33

"BE-ATTITUDES"

"I sit on a bus, feeling like an island as you avoid the seat to either side of me. Finally, when every other seat is taken, you sit down beside me. By then I am tempted to stand or move, just to express my disdain for you.

"I walk into your restaurant and you hustle me, with expert cunning, to an undesirable table next to the kitchen.

"Knowing that I'm not a servant, you suggest the servants' elevator to me—even though I'm wearing my very best suit.

"During one wintry night years ago, I sought shelter in a hotel in up-state New York. The desk clerk ignored me when I asked for a room and pushed the register toward a white youth who stood just behind me. 'But this man was before me,' the young man explained. 'We don't take Negroes in this hotel,' came the clerk's answer. 'Then I wouldn't stay here either,' the young man said, after which he turned, shoved his guitar case beneath his arm and, without a word went back into the cold. If a hotel refused me today, would you do what that boy did?" [1]

Gordon Parks

The following was written by a volunteer worker after a summer in the ghetto of Milwaukee: It's hard. It's vulgar. It's shocking and irreverent. But it does carry a message.

On the first day God made Schlitz and Seagrams.
On the second day God made neon.
On the third day God made the inner city.
On the fourth day God made needles and syringes.

On the fifth day God made lice.
And then on the sixth day, when all was ready, God
  made man.
And God loved man and placed him in the inner city.
And God said increase and multiply and fill the bars
  and the brothels.

And as God was going home from church that
  evening
He took a wrong turn and wound up in the inner city.
And as God was going home from church that evening
He met a young girl who propositioned Him.
And God said haven't you ever heard of God and the
  sixth commandment?
And she said, "Shove the sermon, dad, I can do better
  at the Salvation Army.
I'd really like to stay and talk, but the day is coming
  when no girl can be without work."
And God met a wino, and a pusher, and a pimp, and
  a queer
And then went home and thought a lot
About sending fire or government money, or social
  workers or something equally clever to destroy the
  inner city.
He even thought of sending His Son,
but figured . . . no . . . some cop would see him talking
to a prostitute and run both of them in on a morals
  charge.
Once was enough.

And God said I will come and live in the inner city.
I will live there till the end of time, if this should be
  the need.
I will hide myself in such a disguise that they will see

35

  my works but not my face: no cross, no cassock.
I will serve them and listen to them and talk with them.
I will get lice.
Together we will do, then talk, of jobs and food and
  rent and books and dignity.
Later, perhaps much later, they will say:
He loves us . . . let us make him our God.
Then I shall be tempted to drop the disguise.
But instead, I shall keep silence
Till they *demand;* Show us your God!

  And I shall say to them: He lives in all men!
Do not leave the inner city. Go farther into it.
Come, let us look together.
We shall find Him wherever men suffer, wherever men
love.
In deep disguise from far within the inner city
I will be their God and they will be my People.

President Kennedy said:

  "We are confronted primarily with a moral issue.
It is as old as the scriptures and it is as clear as the
American Constitution. Whether we are going to treat
our fellow Americans as we want to be treated. If an
American, because his skin is dark, cannot eat lunch
in a restaurant open to the public, if he cannot send
his children to the best public schools available, if he
cannot vote for the public officials to represent him, if,
in short, he cannot enjoy the full and free life which
all of us want, then who among us would be content
to have the color of his skin changed and stand in his

place? Who among us would then be content with the counsels of patience and delay?"

Martin Luther King had a dream that "One day this nation will rise up and live out the true meaning of its creed: 'We hold these truths to be self-evident that all men are created equal.'"

We've come a long way since 1878 to realizing that dream, as you can tell from the following advertisement taken from a newspaper clipping of a sale held in Woodford County, Kentucky.

"SALE"

"Having sold my farm and I am leaving for Oregon Territory by ox team, will offer on March 1, all of my personal property, to wit:

"All ox teams except two teams, Buck and Tom and Jerry; 2 milk cows; 1 gray mare and colt; 1 pair of oxen and yoke; 1 baby yolk; 2 ox carts; 1 iron feet of poplar weather boards; plow with wooden moldboard; 1,500 ten-feet fence rails; 1 60 gallon soap kettle; 85 sugar troughs, made of white ash timber; 10 gallons of maple syrup; 2 spinning wheels; 30 pounds of mutten tallow; 1 large loom made by Jerry Wilson; 300 poles; 100 split hoops; 100 empty barrels; 1 32-gallon barrel of Johnson Miller whiskey, 7 years old; 20 gallons of apple brandy; 1 40-gallon still of oak-tanned leather; 1 dozen real books; 2 handle hoods; 3 scythes and cradles; 1 dozen wooden pitchforks; one-half interest in tan yard; 1 32-calibre rifle; bullet mold and powder

37

horn, rifle made by Ben Miller; 50 gallons of soft
soap; hams, bacon and lard, 40 gallons sorghum molas-
ses; 6 head fox hounds, all soft-mouthed except one.

"At the same time I will sell my six negro slaves—2
men, 65 and 50 years old; 2 boys, 12 and 18 years old;
2 mulatto wenches, 40 and 30 years old. Will sell all
together to same party. Will not separate them.

"Terms of sale: Cash in hand, or note to draw 4
per cent interest with Bob McConnel as surety.

"My home is two miles south of Versailles, Ky., on
the McCouns Ferry Pike. Sale begins at 8 o'clock.
Plenty to eat and drink." P. L. Moss

Finally, if President Kennedy called the racial
problem a moral issue, and if morals have to do
with one's relationship to another, and if Christ said
to love one another ... *where have all the Christians
gone?* It reminds me of what Mahatma Gandhi said:
"I like your Christ, but I don't like your Christians."

By the way, what color was Christ? No one has
ever said . . . .

1. Courtesy LIFE magazine, (c) 1968 Time Inc.

The Drug Addict

"He shall lead me by flowing streams and make me lie down in green pastures." Ps 22

JESUS WAS A MAN totally alive. He smelled the rose and tasted the wine. He loved the solitude of the mountain and the power of the sea. He loved nature, using similes and metaphors from the birds of the air to the waving wheat in the fields.

Jesus was a man utterly *free*. He had no home, few possessions, he walked all over Palestine. When telling his followers what his way of life was like, he said: "Be not anxious about what you are to eat, or wear. Your heavenly father who takes care of the birds of the air and feeds them, knows you need these things. And aren't you of much greater value than they?" His attitude toward this world's good things was one of gratitude. He never was possessed by them, never grasped and clung to any material good. And this made him free ... for when one cannot bring himself to give away something he possesses, he in turn is possessed by that thing.

Just before his passion, Jesus reminded Simon Peter of how good he had it when they lived and worked together:

> "Did you go in want of anything, when I sent you out without purse or wallet or shoes?" They told him, "Nothing." Lk 22:36

Jesus lived every moment of this life ... turned on. He lived as if he really meant what he said: "I am the life!" He was so excited about life ... not in a jumping-up-and-down way, but in such a deep and thoroughly physical and spiritual way that he truly acted immortal.

Jesus was a man who could have wielded tremendous political and social power. His platform and policy was love ... and for that he was kicked, spit at, mocked, shoved, beaten and finally murdered ... all because he chose to love.

He was a powerful man. I can't possibly imagine him standing talking to those crowds meekly wringing his hands, and quietly, in a Casper Milquetoast way saying in a mousy voice: "If you want to be my follower love one another, as I have loved you! I have come to bring my peace to the world. Not as the world gives, but as I give."

I can see him shouting this at his impatient followers. I can see the blood rush up his strong face, and distend the veins in his neck as he said: "If you want to follow me ... take up your cross daily and follow me. Love one another!" (John Kennedy said it in a different way: "Ask not what your country can do for you, ask what you can do for your country.")

Many of today's youth are being alienated from materialism because they're smart enough to see it doesn't offer all the happiness its cracked up to give. Madison Avenue uses *Playboy, Life,* and even *Better Homes and Gardens* to give the image of today's happiest American couple as having two bright healthy kids (a boy and a girl of course), a neat $30,000 house in the suburbs, a boat, and God knows what else. But kids coming from many of these middle-class, ulcer-ridden, debt-filled, divorce-smashed homes are saying, "Nuts! I don't want any part of this."

Turning on, tuning in and dropping out is just a violent reaction to materialism. Drugs are used as a kind of vehicle to get away from a superficial life. I had a police officer talk to the group and later invited a reformed drug addict come in to address the class. Her opening line to them was: "I am a drug addict." When the students closed their mouths and regained their composure, she then proceeded to tell them, that she hasn't used drugs for eight years, but

41

lived through twelve years of hell before that on all kinds of drugs from Demerol to Benzedrine.

She used the phrase, "Now I know what the really reallies are!" Here are some of her "Really Reallies":

1. "I was a pathological liar."
2. "I would have done anything. I would have slept with anyone. The pills were my only god."
3. "It doesn't matter what you do, or what happens to you, an addict has no choice."
4. "I had to completely let go of my daughter."
5. "I doubt if you'll find a virgin among grass-smokers."
6. Re: Pushers: "They are the lowest form of life. I have no use for them."
7. "You can't buy instant maturity in a pill. You have to earn it."
8. "I didn't think there was a thing wrong with me."
9. "Why do teenagers start? Fools."
10. "You'll never find an old addict."
11. "To accept me as I was was hard."
12. "Now I can't hold a resentment against anyone, because somehow they grow."
13. "I feel I began living eight years ago when I got off drugs."

After the students heard the police officer, the

drug addict, and had discussed the problem of the teenager and drugs, wrote the following:

"Drugs seem like such a fruitless escape. If a person is really in need of 'turning on' there are so many ways he can do it which would increase his wholeness instead of diminishing it. Or maybe the problem is that some users want to lose their identity."

"Drugs are not an individual matter. A lot of talk is going around right now about being a number in society. I don't agree with this. If you're going to think you're a number, then you've created the situation. If you know you're not a number, then you can accept the modern world without having to escape. If persons, individual persons, could only see the value of themselves they would not take drugs to escape."

Other students wrote in all honesty:

"I really don't know where to begin. Drug addiction is a very frightful subject. But drugs in general, offer a lot for us to learn. You can read books and more books about drugs, but it's just like everything else. To really understand something you have to experience it."

"There is good in drugs and it is obvious to see this. They are used in hospitals to help people who are suffering. And there are several other medical uses for

43

them. Other than this, they are abused. But I don't feel qualified to say much about them, because I don't know that much about them."

"I think there are, however, good uses for such drugs as marijuana that are not medical uses. Because I have used it before, I have a completely different attitude toward it. Before I had tried it I condemned it completely until someone asked me, 'How can you say it's wrong when you don't even know anything about it?' I think this made me realize that I didn't know anything about it and it wasn't fair for me to make a judgment on it. So I read more and more about it and talked to people who had smoked it and I really wanted to try it, not to get kicks or to be 'cool' but because I wanted to know what it was."

"I have no regrets for smoking it and I'll smoke it again if I ever want to. I'm not psychologically addicted. I don't use it as a crutch. For what I get out of it and for what it does to me or rather doesn't do to me, I can see nothing evil or sinful in it for me. I think whether it is wrong or not must be decided by the individual. I can see where it would be harmful to some people. I guess I'm lucky that it didn't hurt me (what I mean is, cause me to depend on marijuana). I question whether it was right for me to take the chance, but then is it right to drive a car? It could hurt you too."

"For me it makes me realize how much time I'm wasting and how really blind we are. We don't see the complexity of life and the world. I'm sure some people have been able to realize these things without

44

using a drug or something, but I didn't and I'm glad I realize this now."

"It's really funny how my views about marijuana changed after I had tried it. Somehow I felt that (and still feel) there was nothing wrong with it and there was something about it that was so wonderful, that I wanted to tell my mother. I was excited like I had really discovered something."

"When I think of what I learned from using marijuana it makes me realize how lucky some people are because they see these things about life that it was so hard for me to understand."

"I don't think you could say I was a juvenile delinquent or a 'mixed up kid' because I smoke pot, I'm just a little more aware than I think I would have been."

Another student says with a little anger in her pen:

"Just what is the world coming to! Just like alcohol, drugs endanger the lives of others. Is that Christian? I would really like to ask someone who has taken L.S.D. or marijuana because of social pressure, to find out why it's so hard to refuse it. I just can't understand it at all. All I can say is, "God please help those who can't help themselves because of their lack of discipline—not for their sake primarily, but for the sake of others.""

"For the sake of others . . . ." Jesus said: "Love

one another." "Love your neighbor as yourself." "Bear one another's burdens." Maybe he had in mind self-discipline in this matter, for the sake of others' physical and psychological welfare.

One perceptive young lady said:

> "We now find ourselves in a permissive society, and many of us do not know how to handle our new found freedom."

She's honest. And how are adults going to help them find out how to handle it? By using their experience and wisdom, by calling in confidence on Christ to help them *show* their children how to use the same freedom offered by Christ and this "permissive society." St. Paul said: "All things are good for me but not all things are expedient."

> "Drugs scare me," one teenager wrote. "Teenagers today are tempted to be on the 'in-group' by playing with drugs. I thank God I have a strong enough will and pray that I won't break down. Christ said that our bodies are temples of the Holy Spirit. To misuse these bodies is wrong! And drugs misuse the body!"

So, what's a teenager to do? Jesus said: "Let him who has eyes to see, see! Let him who has ears to hear, hear!" In other words, be aware of the world your heavenly Father has made for you; and enjoy all the innocent delights he has given you.

Turn on to the world as it is, in its reality, not in an artificial way.

One of the students in a bit of exasperation wrote:

"Why can't people enjoy life naturally instead of taking some drug in order to be 'happy'? It seems to me those who take drugs are trying to escape something. Life is life. I don't believe a person needs L.S.D. or marijuana to 'experience' life, all you have to do is open your eyes!"

One of the better films of our times is called *Occurrence at Owl Creek Bridge*. It describes in detail how a man is being hung for breaking the law. As he is prepared for hanging he is led to a bridge over a river (Owl Creek). A simple board is wedged through the side of the bridge. A soldier-executioner stands on one end, the condemned man on the other. As the condemned man is waiting for the soldier to step off the other end of the board his life seems to pass before him. He sees a log floating downstream, he remembers his wife, Abbey, and his children. He is aware that the sun blinds his eyes.

Then the order is given, the soldier steps off the plank and down he goes with the noose around his neck. Something strange happens, however. The rope somehow breaks and he goes, bound, into the water. He sinks and sinks. Then, realizing he has a chance, he struggles with the bonds on his legs and wrists.

47

He fights for his life to free himself. Slowly and painfully he gets the bonds off and swims to the surface with his lungs exploding. And just as he breaks the surface he lets out a shrill scream, as he takes his first breath of new life! The genius of the director uses this as a sign of birth—as in physical birth the baby cries with the thrill of new life, as in baptism water is used to sign new life—so he now screams with the joy of rebirth.

Fully aware that he does have a second chance at life, he begins to see the details of life. He is aware for the first time that there are leaves on the trees. He can even see the small veins in the leaves. He notices a spider spinning an intricate web and the drops of crystal water on the strands. He notices the cloud formations and is aware of the wetness of the water on his body.

The soldiers begin to shoot at him to complete the execution. So he swims downstream. And as he fights his way through a hail of bullets, past a water snake, and over a waterfall he is finally washed ashore completely exhausted.

Lying on the beach he opens his eyes and sees blood on his hand. He looks at it, smiles, then rolls over and over on the sand for the sheer joy of being alive. Then he spots a flower. He crawls over to it and simply smells it. Sheer joy!

A bullet whistles through the trees and he begins

to run. He runs and runs and his body begins to pain. He falls.—He gets up and runs again. Finally, he arrives at mysterious gates. They open by themselves. He goes through them and finds himself at home. He calls his wife's name and runs toward her with arms outstretched—running, running. And just as he goes to embrace her, the film flashes back to the Owl Creek Bridge and the rope breaks his neck with a chilling snap!

The audience is left stunned. All his struggling and pain and joy . . . all the beauty he had become aware of with his second chance for life is a fantasy that passed through his mind in a second as he dropped to his death.

The lesson learned by the audience is awareness. Awareness of this beautiful world and life around us. So many things we miss in life because we aren't aware. We aren't aware of the smell of the tingling air after a snowfall. We stumble through the day without seeing the change of light and shadow. We aren't aware of the feel of clothes against our back, or the softness of grass under our feet. We eat like robots not enjoying the subtle tastes of different foods.

What dull children we are in this beautiful world our Father has given us! We don't need drugs to heighten our awareness. We need to be turned-on to the million bombardments of our mind and senses that we have every day. Jesus liked to take walks in the mountains. He loved the power of the ever changing, moving sea. He was aware of the birds of the air, the grass in the yards, the lilies of the field. He was a man completely free because he was not dependent on any *thing* to turn him on like a light-switch. He had "no place to lay his head," but he had the whole world as his home. He was free. He was aware. He was totally and wonderfully alive! And that's what Christ can offer the teenager . . . *Life!*

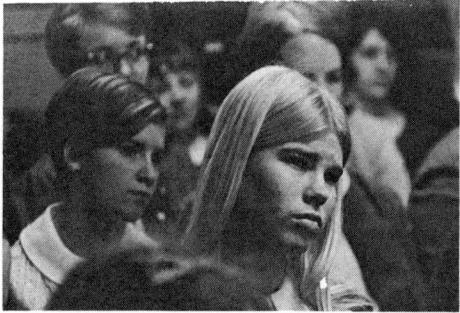

The Alcoholic

ACCORDING TO *Alcohol and Health* (First Special Report to the U.S. Congress from the Secretary of Health, Education and Welfare, Dec. 1971), alcohol is the most abused drug in the United States; and problems related to alcohol and alcoholism are increasing. Problems like crimes, job loss, family breakups, fighting, and personal tragedies.

It is estimated that of the 95 million drinkers in the United States, 9 million men and women are alcohol abusers or alcoholics.

We used to have the idea that alcoholics inhabit the hotels of skid row. No. Only 3 to 5 per cent of the nation's alcoholic population are there. The rest are in the working and homemaking population.

In one recent year alcohol directly contributed to, or caused 28,000 traffic accident deaths. And 6 out of every 10 youths (age 16-24) were drinking or drunk when they died in twisted automobile metal and glass.

Alcohol abuse and alcoholism slugs the economy each year about $15 billion! That's $10 billion in lost work time in business, industry and civilian government. $2 billion in health and welfare services for the alcoholic and his/her family. $3 billion for property damage, medical and related expenses.

One-third of all arrests were for public intoxication. And if disorderly conduct, vagrancy and driving under the influence of alcohol were lumped under "Public Intoxication" the number would jump to around 45 per cent. That's a lot! That's almost half of all arrests!

What a problem! And it's a problem for the Christian. . . .

I took this subject for our religion class because alcohol is a human problem. People suffer because of drink. Jesus was concerned about the sufferings of people—any suffering. Christianity is basically an "I-Thou-We" relationship. We are not rocks. We are not islands. We live with other people, some close to us, others not. What we are will affect other people in one way or another.

Jesus said to love your neighbor as yourself but before you can really love your neighbor you *must* first love yourself. An alcoholic rarely does. I will not go into the physiological, chemical or even psychological causes and cures of alcoholism. I leave that for those who are more qualified. I will simply address myself to the general human problems caused by alcoholism as we studied it in class.

To give the students some preparatory ideas about alcoholism I invited a speaker, an "expert," on the subject, to give the students some basic realistic appraisals and explanations. (It's a sad fact some of the students know more about the consequences of the problem that I do because of someone in their family who is an alcoholic.)

One such expert spoke of 3000 teenagers in Milwaukee who were interviewed as to why they drink. They gave three reasons:

1. Social Pressure: "All my friends drink, Dad. I'd be a square if I didn't."

2. Pretending to be adult: "Who doesn't want to be a swinger like Dean Martin?"

3. Problem solving: "I like to get smashed, because then I can forget my parents and my other problems."

Alcohol is always related to others, either as the cause, the effect or the reason. Jesus said: "Love your neighbor as yourself." This love of self is very important. The teenager needs to feel a pride and respect in himself. It takes a wise parent, and wise teachers to instill this self-respect in a child. Kids who are well-balanced, who have pride in themselves don't "get soaked" for kicks or escape or pretence. They can face life squarely and live.

Always look for the slightest hint of goodness or accomplishment in the teenager, anything that will support him, anything that will encourage him to be self-confident.

An unexpected compliment from a teacher on a good answer or observation in class puts a glow on the student all day; a word of praise for a job well done—anything from cleaning erasers to an assignment done well. A simple "thank you" to a student for a favor shows respect for his existence. Noticing a ribbon in a girl's hair, mentioning a boy's neat appearance—all these things help build a foundation for a healthy love of self.

One of the speakers told the class that an alcoholic cannot have a quiet conversation with another. An alcoholic cannot have a relationship with another. There will be lots of acquaintances but no relationships.

For Christians there must be an "I-Thou-We" relationship to others. "I"—one must know and love oneself as he or she is, not some fantasy of oneself. "Thou"—one must know and love the other person in the same way, as he or she is, not as one would like them to be, or wish they were, but rather as they are. "We"—this love-union of understanding and acceptance forms the basic Christian community, the "We." The philosophy is simple. It is beautiful. It works! But to build such a community is indeed difficult in our present human condition. There are so many variables and subtle forces in the development of each single human being that "programming" of the total person is virtually impossible. One can't "program" respect and pride in oneself—or take a pill to make it grow. Respect and pride come from deep inside oneself and largely from relationships to others, *always* through freedom.

At their stage of development teenagers are frighteningly free, free to be what they want to be. They have energy and enthusiasm and drive to accomplish so many goals, but they have to have the vision to see the goals and the encouragement to pursue them. One of the problems of middle-class life is that the teenager doesn't start out at the bottom of the ladder, but somewhere near the middle or top. Ideally, he has a secure home, good diet, money to spend. Materially he is comfortable. But unlike the less-advantaged teenager he has no incentive to really push toward a dream.

One of the dangers of such a middle-class condition is that one can grow up without self-discipline—a self-discipline that supports from *the inside*. The middle-class kid can have a car; he can have access to liquor; he can transport himself in a matter of an hour on our superhighways in a super-car to an environment that is super-undisciplined. The guiding lines of the home are not there, the pressure of community respect are gone and he is free to do what he wishes, at least as long as he doesn't break the law and get caught by the police.

Here is where the teenager begins to drink. He drinks beer, wine, and hard liquor. It's easy to get because his diet, the PE program at school, even his genetic make-up and a whole raft of other variables make many teenagers look older than they are. Besides who's going to argue with a kid over a 6-pack of beer if he can make some money!

Of course, one of the biggest dangers in teenage drinking is driving a two-ton package of steel. When the teenager is loaded, the car becomes a leathal weapon. Statistics on how many deaths have been caused by teenage drinking speak of the seriousness of the problem.

The Mobil Gas Company puts out an ad that chillingly tells the teenager that drinking and driving don't mix. It encourages a girl to refuse to go home with a boy who has been drinking, to call a taxi, to call home for a ride, or even to call the police to take her home. The ad says that it would be worth a little embarrassment not to have a pretty face cut up and scarred for life because it went through the windshield of a car driven by a boy who had been drinking.

Now all this may sound like rattling bones in the haunted house, but to me it is basically Christian to respect oneself as a body-person, physically and spiritually—and also to respect the other person. Alcohol *can* lessen one's respect for himself or herself. How? Well, very subtly. It starts in the opposite way with the false feeling of superiority on the part of the teenager acting "like an adult." Then after the first few real benders the teenager experiences real hangovers in the morning. The heavy sick feeling that makes one want to pull the covers over his head and quietly withdraw from the world. Many a life-time of drinking has begun in this fashion.

How important that at this stage the teenager should have been prepared with a right attitude toward drink. This attitude must be nurtured in early life. In Germany, for example, young people can drink beer in public and they don't seem to have a major problem with alcoholism. This is true in part at least because their attitude toward drink has been tempered with proper discipline. Liquor does not have the fascination there that it does here in the United States where laws make it enticing, like the apple in the Garden of Eden.

"BE-ATTITUDES"

Alcoholism is America's no. 4 problem child. It affects 6.5 million people directly—and God knows how many indirectly. It is called a "family sickness" because for every alcoholic an average of at least four other people are affected adversely ... "love your neighbor as yourself." Like many fatal diseases, alcoholism has mysterious and subtle beginnings. Linked to the physical predispositions which is hereditary there is always the added element of acquired habit. Non-drinkers do not become alcoholics.

The following stories are cited as examples of what *can* happen if drinking grows to alcoholism. These stories concern alcoholic parents and remember, teenagers are just a few short years away from parenthood.

The first story is about two teenagers, a boy and a girl, who come home to find their mother drunk on the couch. The girl had her boy-friend with her and was embarrassed to have to support her mother upstairs to bed in front of him. The girl didn't go to school the rest of the week because she was so upset. The boy was furious, and heartsick and cried. The mother's drinking got worse and worse, because alcoholism grows progressively worse as time goes on.

The son began to stay away from home more and more. The daughter didn't go out on dates because she couldn't bear having any boy-friend see her mother drunk. The father became increasingly short-tempered and began to beat up his wife causing the children to be more upset and disgusted. The daughter would try to stay with her mother so that she wouldn't feel alone, and therefore wouldn't drink to drown her loneliness. But she was always coming across things like vodka in a "mouthwash" bottle, a bottle of gin hidden in the pantry.

She told me, "I used to get furious at mom, pour alcohol down the sink, and give her awful lectures." Then she'd ask, not fully understanding her mother's problem, "How could she do this to me if she really loved me? Sometimes I think *we* drove her to drink because we didn't love her enough."

A friend of hers introduced her to the organization called "Alateens," which is an organization for teenagers who have alcoholic parents. It helps them by mutual support of other teenagers (so important at this stage of life), to be less self-conscious, less fearful and more open and understanding.

In this particular case the mother did seek help and the story has a happy ending. But for so many that, unfortunately, isn't true.

I can't help but think that when Jesus said "to give drink to the thirsty" he may have had in mind the alcoholic. But he didn't mean "drink" literally. He meant to give the "drink" of understanding, concern, help and support to someone who is psychologically or spiritually "thirsting" for self-identity, or self-pride, or security.

Alcoholism is a human gap-filler. Jesus was very wise to tell us to love ourselves. If we really did then we would not need artificial supports for courage or self-identity.

The second story was written in a letter published by *Reader's Digest* (Nov. '66). The letter was addressed by a father to his teenage son. It is a poignant letter, a letter that tells of heartbreak and sorrow, of physical pain and spiritual pain caused by a man's selfishness. One of the important parts of the letter is the father's explanation of how it all started. He says: "Then how do we get to be drunks? Some people think we become alcoholics from drinking too much. I think we drink too much because we had something wrong with us in the first place and used alcohol as a crutch. We had the equivalent of a broken leg in our inner selves—a weakness, a fear, a sense of anxiety, a shadow of uncertain outline that dogged our steps. This is not unusual in itself, especially among young people as they are becoming adults. Alcohol is a crutch. I picked up my crutch in the most innocent way. Some buddies of mine and I would get a keg of beer on Saturday afternoon. We had a good time, had fun. I didn't realize it then, but I enjoyed beer too much. I would go from the "social drinker" to the "drunken kid" very, very often.

"After I got out of school I looked for friends who liked to drink. Your mother liked to drink—or at least she thought she did. She made a vain attempt to keep up with me, but then she found herself on a bobsled ride so familiar to wives of alcoholics. From enjoying our life together she shifted to tolerating it, and then to rebelling against it. She tried to understand me, to help me, and her only reward was a kick in the teeth. The divorce itself was an anticlimax. Our marriage had ended long before. I was just an overgrown adolescent."[1]

The father then goes on to tell of different classes of alcoholics—how they got started, how much they drink, etc., and some tell-tale signs of the beginnings of alcoholism. He ends the letter by saying:

"You will have problems in your life. You will have disappontments, doubts and fears. Try never to make the mistake of seeking an artificial, temporary solution to those problems through alcohol, pills or narcotics. A way of life cannot be built on such flights from reality...."

And this is my point. Christianity is a way of life. It is a way of life that centers around a person, Jesus Christ. He gave us attitudes toward life. He showed us how to live—completely "turned on" to life —he told us how to "Be." His "Be-attitude" is to live

61

life to the full. And this means hurting sometimes. This means crying sometimes. This means laughing sometimes. This means pleasure sometimes. But always it means *living* in the fullest sense of the word.

Alcohol can lead to a deterioration of life. By its chemical make-up even, it is a depressant. Alcohol can be the cause of pain, spiritual and physical, to others, needless pain, selfish pain. If it is, a Christian hurts other people, and therefore, sins.

The use of alcohol in moderation is a different story. Jesus tasted wine. He was a man of passionate enthusiasm, yet a man of moderation. I cannot imagine him selfishly using any of his Father's creatures to excess.

To help us understand alcoholism and the alcoholic the class went downtown to "Pioneer Fellowship House" which is an organization established to help the alcoholic. On their brochure they say about the Pioneer House that is "warmly humanitarian." It is "founded on faith and conviction, faith in God and conviction of the ultimate goodness of man. We believe that, with the righ kind of help, man can rise from the depths—that man can change for the better. We believe that life was meant to be worthwhile and a rewarding experience. We believe these things because we see them happening, . . . step by step by step."

One of the students wrote this after visiting Pioneer Fellowship House:

"Actually, I feel about the same way about alcohol as I do about drugs. I haven't really heard a logical reason for this kind of escape. Perhaps this is because there really isn't a logical reason.

"I wish everyone could see a film we saw in drivers' training. It showed a human brain being dissected. Actually, it compared the brain of a healthy person and an alcoholic. The difference was unbelievable. The convolutions were distorted and the brain discolored. It was really in terrible shape.

"It also showed the effects of alcohol which appear immediately such as the loss of inhibitions and motor control. It seems really bad that anyone would actually be willing to sacrifice his dignity for whatever pleasure drinking can give.

"It seems that the further we go in this course, the more complicated the problems become because if a person has one he seems prone to have two or more other problems. For instance, Miss Adamek told us that one of the big reasons for drinking is personal problems. Now when we look at some of the homeless, we can see that either alcohol could have caused their homelessness or their homelessness could have driven them to alcohol. For example, a father has to show his manhood someway, and in the the subculture of poverty, this means drinking.

"It was really very hard for me to be sympathetic to alcoholics because it is so much the person's fault. Now, I think I am beginning to see a little bit better

63

that sometimes circumstances overpower the individual. I can't yet erase all of my feelings of condemning the alcoholic. Maybe, someday I'll be able to condemn only the reasons for alcoholism."

Teenagers today have a refreshing understanding of people, and a tolerance for their problems. Maybe it's because they are so exposed to so many by way of television and movies. The movie industry today is advocating a new frankness for the sake of realism, and while it can be offensive at times, there is supreme value in meeting life head-on, in seeing life as it is.

One student wrote:

"I am disappointed because I didn't get everything out of this that I could have. Maybe I should blame myself, but somehow alcoholism seems so distant in my life that I didn't really have anything concrete to hold on to. I've never really known it, or seen its effects on anyone very close to me. But still, I can't see what *I* have to do. I don't really think Christianity has anything to do with the problems of alcoholism. No one really considers it a Christian question of whether: 'Well am I being a Christian, as far as others are concerned, because I have a few drinks on the weekends?' I mean kids just don't look that far ahead to think: 'Will this affect my later life? Could I become an alcoholic?'

"I don't really know what else to say. I want to understand the problem. I have had little experience with it. I'm still very confused as to where Christianity fits in."

I feel as long as this student has the question in her mind now, later on she will get the answers. As her life-experience grows, as she meets more people, as she sees how individual human lives intermingle and interact on one another—then alcoholism will be seen in the context of loving one's neighbor as oneself.

One "expert" on the problem told the students that one alcoholic effects fourteen people with his problem. In the home there is the most hurt—constant quarreling, divorce, broken families, a family with a father with no job; juvenile maladjustment of all kinds, and so on and on.

Another student said:

> "I think the Louis Martin Home for Alcoholics is wonderful. They help each other and themselves. And this raises the question again: 'Is alcoholism a Christian problem, or a human problem?' I think love should motivate us to help. But this love is natural, not necessarily Christian. I mean who wouln't help out an alcoholic father or mother or brother or sister? Anyone would do that. You don't have to be a Christian.
>
> "I think its *more* of a Christian duty, however, to help because of Christ's attitude toward helping people who are in need."

Alcoholism is a problem for all classes of people, all races, colors and creeds. When Jesus had "compassion on the multitudes" as we so often read in the

65

"BE-ATTITUDES"

Gospels, I can't help but think as he sees this problem today, he has the same compassion. The Christian must be Christ today, to have understanding and compassion toward those who suffer from the agony of alcoholism.

1. Excerpt from "An Alcoholic's Letter to His Son," The Reader's Digest, November 1966. Copyright 1966 by The Reader's Digest Assn., Inc.

The Handicapped

A LADY TOLD ME once that President Kennedy did more to help people understand mental retardation during his two years in office than had previously been done in the last fifty years. At that time people considered the mentally retarded as people to be hidden from society. The hospitals and institutions were built out in the country, many times with fences around them. The medical care was minimal and done heroically by relatively few people.

Unless a person has a mentally handicapped member in his family he can go along in life with little concern for them, so I decided in the class to try to help my students understand the mentally retarded by going out to Fircrest School for the mentally handicapped in Seattle. In many ways it was the most rewarding experiences we had during the entire course.

I was a little apprehensive about taking these

antiseptic teenagers through Fircrest. It was my own non-understanding that the people there were persons. I had never had the problem in my own family, so was unaware of it, too.

As we drove up to the gate we saw one man who looked to be about thirty staring through a fence. No one paid attention to him. Then we went to the superintendent's office where a lady explained the set-up of Fircrest to us, how the people were fed and clothed and housed by the State, how they were understaffed, overworked and underpaid. Yet she wasn't bitter. She just stated the fact and shrugged her shoulders as if she really didn't care too much about the money.

Then she led us on a tour of the grounds and building. We met men and women who were boys and girls mentally—very friendly in most cases, in other cases seemingly unaware of life around them. One man endeared himself to the students when he came up to the group, said, "Hi," and proceeded to gently shake hands with each and everyone. He called himself "uncle," and proudly showed everyone his new watch. He was instant love. He broke the ice for us to be more relaxed ... from what, I don't know ... I guess fear of the unknown, preconceived ideas about the mentally handicapped, etc., etc.

Anyway we proceeded to a ward or cottage of "Senior girls" who were so delighted to see all of us and wanted to show us their stuffed animals their families had given them, a holy picture, a new bedspread—all the things that delight the hearts of children.

Mrs. Russell mentioned one girl whom we saw as having made such great progress, because she said, people were concerned about her. She advanced from a self-centered, frightened, mentally and physically handicapped girl to a relaxed, outgoing happy person who finally realized people loved her. Farther on the tour we went into a cottage that housed the severely retarded. I discovered that these were the people who were the most loved. They were the most handicapped. They had to stay in bed all day, everyday—except when they would be taken out to exercise their limbs, and to change their body positions. Here were the hydrocephalics, and the crippled, those who had no control over their body movements, and those who laid motionless always.

As we walked through this ward the students were very quiet. They had never seen anything like this before in their lives. Some of the patients would make guttural noises as if groaning, but they were apparently trying to express themselves. Others would merely lie motionless. They were brought to a halt when they saw a little boy and a little girl who lay motionless because of their large heads. These were the hydrocephalics. To be perfectly honest the students were taken aback and startled for a moment. But I was even more taken aback and startled to see how warm and gentle the students were. One of the nurses talked to the little girl in the bed, whose head was as big as her body, and she smiled back and showed the students her ring. One of the students then walked up to her, took her hand and made a loving fuss (as women do) over her new ring. The other followed and soon the students had spread out all through that sad ward to talk to the patients.

Their bodies were deformed. Some of them had no muscular control over their head and had to wear football helmets to keep from bumping their heads. Others had socks on their hands so that they would not scratch their faces with their fingernails. Some were lying on mattresses on the floor and had to be turned over on their sides occasionally so they would have a variety and a change of body position. The rooms were painted gay but soft colors of blue and white and pink. The nurses had hung mobiles from the ceiling so that the patients could follow them with their eyes.

In an older men's ward I remember seeing a color television set with the picture rolling over and over because the vertical hold was not set properly. Those men were fascinated by the color and movement and the nurse told us that even that was enjoyable for them.

Just before we went into one of the cottages the

lady who was conducting our tour told us not to be shocked or surprised at the severity of the patients' mental or physical handicap. She said they are all individual persons worth our care and concern. Then she mentioned something that I never forgot. "Look at their eyes. They have beautiful eyes." When we got into the ward we did see some cases of severe mental and physical retardation, but I can remember seeing the eyes of one little girl. I'll never forget her. She was standing with her hands on a little chair trying so hard to look at the students but she couldn't keep her little head up very long because of her weak and uncontrollable neck muscles. But as she looked at us, one of the students said: "Look at her eyes, Mr. Farley. Aren't they beautiful?" They were. They were brown, and the whites of them were pure and unblemished. And her hair was soft and dark brown and hung loosely on her shoulders. If an artist wanted to paint innocence, that little girl would be the perfect subject.

While the patients at Fircrest elicited an outgoing feeling of concern and love, we were all in awe of the dedicated people who took care of them. They were terribly understaffed. In one ward there were thirty husky youngsters and only three people on duty to take care of them. Most of them were in diapers and many had no control over their bowels. They had to be changed regularly. They had to be taken in wheel chairs to a bathing room where the nurses had to lift them into specially designed tubs. They had to be hand fed, because they couldn't feed themselves. It was a long day of hard work. There are few people who love others as much as those nurses and attendants do.

And there are few people who work as hard for other people.

This was a very important lesson we learned. No matter how "out of shape" the patients were, either mentally or physically, they still were uniquely themselves, persons, individuals. Someone on the staff reminded us of that. He said, "Don't forget, these patients may not look like the rest of society, but always remember they are individual human beings worthy of our respect and concern and love just like anyone else." It's incredible, but true, that we would have to be reminded of that.

In the Gospels Jesus had compassion and concern for the man "possessed" and for an epileptic or spastic boy who had no muscular or bodily control. He went out of his way to stop and cure the woman with the uncontrollable flow of blood. Lepers, who were social outcasts came to him in droves to be cured. Jesus associated himself with the less fortunate in society. He recognized in each single individual a uniqueness and had concern for each one, for example the blind man shouting from the side of the road,

"Jesus, Son of David, have mercy on me" The Apostles angrily tried to silence him, but Jesus stopped and walked through the milling crowd to the poor man and asked what he could do for him. "Lord that I may see," was his plea. Jesus quietly replied, "I will it. Receive your sight." Jesus wasn't "too busy," too taken up with the pressures of business, to be concerned about the individual. We, too, must be aware of the individual in society if we are to be Christians. To be a Christian means to bring the love of Christ to all men, especially to those most in need.

After our visit to Fircrest school we had plenty of material to discuss in class to get a perspective on what a Christian attitude should be toward the mentally and physically handicapped. The comments and observations of the students were very interesting. To start off one of the discussions a boy raised his hand and said: "I can't see how those people contribute anything to society. And besides that, they cost a lot of money to take care of. So why don't we do away with them!"

With that, the roof practically came off the place! I admit I was taken back a few giant steps, but continued to listen as the students talked. One said:

"The first step in being a Christian is knowing how to love others. If you can't love the children at Fircrest,

73

and really believe they have a right to live, then I don't see how you can call yourself a Christian."

Some were charging mad that he would even think such a thing.

"How would you like it, if you had some physical or mental handicap and someone arbitrarily decided to take your life!"

"I think that's a terrible thing to say."

And so on. But the boy who made the suggestion had really never thought of the problem before and he was just verbalizing what first came into his mind. Actually these seventeen-year-olds got down pretty deep into basic human relationships and Christians response.

"Day after day those of us fortunate enough to be physically and mentally normal and fit, wander about this world, *looking* but not really *seeing* the handicapped. We can't see how they are starving for security, affection, and self-worth.

"It wasn't until we went to Fircrest and the Cerebral Palsy Center that we began *seeing* a very real part of our world, the handicapped. It wasn't until we saw the little pin-head boy wheeling the hydrocephalic child in his wheelchair that we realized the unfulfilled needs *every* individual has. As we entered the wards and noticed the little girl holding on to her cold, plastic,

74

unreal security (a doll), waiting for the mere touch of a human hand of affection, we realized that as Christians we must do more than just *see* we must also *act* to help these people. We must give a little bit of ourselves, our love, and our security to make them feel more like persons.

"When we think of the handicapped we tend to think only of those mentally or physically deformed, but the institutions can't hold those who are spiritually or socially deformed. Many people right here around us have no belief whatsoever, no real basis for life, except pleasure maybe. There are also those without friendship or the desire to fulfill their ambitions in life. We must learn to see these individuals as well as those obviously handicapped and go out to them as well. We must become 'other-directed' instead of 'self-directed.'"

Another student said:

"On my trip to visit and tour Fircrest, I had no opportunity to observe how an unfortunate group of human beings exist from day to day in their same retarded state. It was a very different experience for me because I never realized that so many people existed this way. I guess I was like so many others who are so caught up in their own problems and self-centered world that I never cared or wanted to care about them. It is an experience, that has taught me a lesson I will never forget.

"Before my trip to Fircrest, I always took for granted my physical and mental health as if I deserved it. But since then, a day hasn't gone by that I haven't thanked God for my health. My father thinks it is one of the best experiences that has happened to his some-what sheltered little daughter, and it probably is. I'm glad that he encouraged me to go because I did know that there were such people, but seeing them is an entirely different matter. It shocked me into the reality that these 'vegetables' are human beings. I don't think people can understand or be sympathetic towards these people until they see them. That's what shocked me—seeing them. (Seeing is believing)."

Some did not want to go to Fircrest and I didn't force them. Some went to a Cerebral Palsy Center not too far from school. At this Center the poor people who have Cerebral Palsy, who can't control their muscles, are taught skills to help them pride themselves as a contributing member of society. One girl wrote this:

"This visit to the Cerebral Palsy Center made a very strong impression on me. Ever since I could understand about people who are handicapped I have felt very deeply about them. It always makes me very mad when people make fun of those who are physically or mentally different. It seems to me people only say those things because handicapped people can't help what they are and can't fight back. I used to feel a deep sympathy for the handicapped but now I feel they need sympathy least of all. They are trying to fit themselves into our society. This I saw very clearly at the Cerebral Palsy Center. They were adding their contributions as little as it might be to society and they were proud that they could.

"I feel most people's closed eyes to the handicapped situation isn't intentional. They just don't understand fully or they just never stop to think about it. People will see handicapped on the street and maybe say, 'Oh, the poor *thing*.' It never clicks in their minds that these 'things' are people just like everybody else and they can help. Even indirectly, by donations no matter how small, if not directly by volunteering their time.

"I myself would very much like to volunteer but there is always something else to do. Sometimes it's important and most of the time it isn't, but it isn't that I don't care because I do. I just can't impress it hard enough into my brain. It just hasn't affected my life strongly enough yet. But it has affected me insofar as I would like to make helping the handicapped my career. I have a very strong feeling for children especially those whom I could help become an active person of society by teaching them to walk with crippled legs or manipulate stiff fingers. Through physical therapy I can fulfill this desire, maybe not now in my crowded life but in the very near future."

To face mental and physical retardation is not an easy task. When we have to suffer we don't like it. We don't like it when we see others suffering. In the case of the mentally and physically handicapped they do not suffer as we think they do. Many of them know they are "different," and when "normal" people stare at them or whisper about them they do suffer mentally. As one person said, "I don't like to go out, because we're different, and the other people notice us."

"BE-ATTITUDES"

One of the students could not face up to the fact some people were mentally and physically handicapped. She had been to Fircrest before and the memories were not pleasant. So she told me she preferred not to go on the trip and asked me if she could stay at school when we went on the trip. I said, "certainly."

She wrote the following:

"I just sat alone
In the classroom.
I wouldn't go.
You wouldn't go either
If you were me and saw
What I saw.
I'll never go back.
I hope it's not bad
To feel this way, but —
The trouble is,
They're human.
You can't know what it's like
Until you've been there.
Some of them are all right
To look at, and maybe even
Fun to play or work with.
Maybe you can understand,
When one of them grabs your arm or leg
And starts crying real tears —
You don't know why,
Or even if they do.
There's one on the floor

Chained to a pillar.
And with a faraway look in his eyes
That stares right through your soul.
There are four or five
Running around screaming, and
A couple in straight jackets
For biting the others and chewing
Their own fingers.
All you want to do is
Crawl in a hole,
Or run away,
Or scream, or just anything except be there.
When you're gone you can't forget.
It's like a nightmare,
And it's real,
And you know it.
When people say we should kill them:
They don't know the difference anyway,
It hurts—because you're not sure.
No one really can be.
But maybe they do know.
Then we'd have to treat them
Like other people.
There are some who could do it —
God knows about them.
But for some people—they're just too different."

Young people of today can be very deep. If we
get the radio shut off, the T.V. blanked-out, get the
food out of their mouths, and stop them from wiggling
long enough to sit down and talk seriously, they startle

the older generation by their depth. One student in this same class said the following,

"I'm a little envious of the people at Fircrest. They may have it a little rougher, but they still can be happy. We worry about whether we watch J. P. Patches with our little sisters or get to watch the latest horror movie. We're pretty selfish when you come down to it, but the question is how do we break out. How do you stop worrying about yourself in a world that keeps reminding you to 'get a good education. Join the Army. Go out and make a buck.' I don't think we are all that selfish, many of us are lazy and don't want to be inconvenienced. I wonder who *really* is deformed, them or us. They have so much less than we do but we are the ones who complain."

When you come right down to it, the mentally and physically handicapped do not need us as much as we need them to keep us human and loving and Christian.

Another student observes:

"Girls go on and on about things like long fingernails or having a face like Julie Christie, or a body like Twiggy or Sophia Loren or straight teeth. They get all upset because they don't get all A's in school or they can't play the piano or draw well. When you think of these people going on and on talking about such stupid, shallow things, and then you look at the people at Fircrest and the Cerebral Palsy Center, you could just kill yourself for ever even thinking of such things, much less talking about them.

"I don't know if I could go and work at either of those places. I am rather afraid, and even a tiny bit repelled by those people. I think, though, that if I kept going to help I could more or less condition myself to see beyond the deformities and see the person."

The physically and mentally handicapped are God's special "in-group." They don't have the ordinary human creature comforts. And, unfortunately, in our society this is a handicap when it comes to their being accepted by others. I wonder if our American image of the "Ideal," the beautiful girl in the Jantzen Sweater and the handsome boy in the Levi stretch pants, isn't distorting the Christian idea of life-values. I think it is. When you come down to it, the slick covered magazines of our society a la *Playboy, Seventeen, Life,* etc., are shaping many of the ideas of our youth. Theirs is the phony world of the unreal. Nobody, but *nobody,* can look as unwrinkled as the models in a glamour magazine. So when we face the reality of human life we must face the wrinkles around the eyes, the blemishes on the cheeks, crooked teeth and flabby middle. And we must also face the reality of the mentally and physically handicapped.

They are people, God's people, just as you and I. He has a special love for them. So should we.

The Aged

THE CHRISTIAN TEENAGER and the aged. Strange subject to take in a Religion class. What's the story? I think our age of mod clothes, jet travel and super cars leaves little room for the shawl, the shuffling walk, or the stutterings of old age. And that's precisely why it is necessary for us as Christians to be concerned about the aged—because the world isn't.

Older people are persons who have lived through their teenage years, young adulthood, and the prime of their life under circumstances very different from our own. Many have had to haul in wood, bake bread in the oven, go "out back" to the bathroom, light kerosene lamps for light. They suffered cold in winter and heat in the summer without central temperature control. They suffered in many areas where we don't because we have the advantage of recent medical advances.

Look at the whole thrust of advertising. It all

aims at the young. They even changed the name of *Olds*-mobile to *Young*-mobile to help sell the image. Some women complain that they can't find a dress to wear because they are all "mini" and young girls are the only ones who can wear them. Some of the most interesting ads, the kind that you whistle and hum, are the ones with the young sound. "We're in the Pepsi generation," "Think young," "The young sound." A tire company has an old lady driving a racy sports car in quiet humor about the liveliness of her old age.

Now I'm not saying we should not "think young," nor, however, should we forget the old. I remember reading a poem that spoke of youth as *not* a time of life . . .

> "Youth is not a time of life
> It is a state of mind
> It is not a matter of ripe cheeks
> Red lips and supple knees;
> It is a temper of the will,
> A quality of the imagination,
> A vigor of the emotions;
> It is a freshness of the deep spring of life."

Does our culture have respect for the aged? Granted that the elderly are often not in the mainstream of life. They may reach a point where their children must decide what should be done for them, should they be put in a nursing home, old folks home, senior citizens residence, or convalescent home? Even though these places do provide at least the minimum comfort, they can also be excuses for shelving one's responsibility towards his parents.

I wonder how Jesus treated his grandparents, Joachim and Anne? Did he get to visit them? Would he talk with them around the fire? Did he bring them little gifts? Did they live close by where he could stop in for lunch amid the hectic pace of his public life? I can't imagine him doing otherwise.

The Gospel writers took great pains to point out Jesus' concern for the old, the crippled and the feeble. For example, he stopped to cure the old woman who had a "flow of blood." He quieted the shaking of the palsied man; he cured the twisted flesh of the man with the "withered hand"; he had compassion on the widow of Naim and brought back to life her only son. Our Lady was probably in her late fifties when Jesus from the cross asked John to take care of her.

Every person to him was important and unique, with individual wants and needs. He always showed a concern about caring for others. This was his "Beattitude" toward the old.

One of the saddest pictures I have ever seen appeared in *Life* magazine. It was of two old people, short, overweight and slow of step, carrying a shopping bag full of their belongings, being escorted from the Berlin Wall by a guard with a rifle on his back, a poignant picture of the helplessness of old age coupled with a denial of their personal freedom. I remember, also, an ad for Japan Airlines where an old Japanese couple are sitting together. They have a serene smile on their faces, and beneath the picture there is the caption: "Come to Japan where old age is beautiful."

Yes, old age can be beautiful. One of my students was assigned in his Junior year to work eight hours a quarter in an old folk's home. At first he didn't like the idea, but since he had no other choice, he went and asked the manager if he could help out. The manager was delighted and asked if he would help an old man who couldn't see or write very well, to write his letters. So he did. The days passed and they became friends. The student began to love the old man because the old man was gentle to him. He had a sense of humor and, because he was an old sailor, had endless sea stories to tell. During one of the conversations in class about old people a student suggested that old people were "out of it." This particular student who had befriended the old man, spoke up in their defense with a touch of anger in his voice. "They're interesting and enjoyable. You just have to be interested in them." His eight hour assignment for class developed into a permanent friendship. The young man visits his old friend frequently still, and both lives have been enriched because of this encounter of youth and old age.

Teenagers have a natural warmth toward older people that is beautiful to see. In order to understand the problems of old age better, our class visited an old people's home near school.

As the class and I walked in, the staff split us up for our tour of the place. The boys went to the men's section, the girls to the women's. The natural charm of the students immediately broke the ice and the old people were ebullient in welcoming them. Some were hard of hearing and shouted when they talked. The kids loved it! Some could not talk and simply put out their hands and grasped the hands of the students. One girl said she almost cried when an old lady took her hand and began to cry for the sheer joy of having someone come to visit her and be interested in her.

This is the basic problem with regard to the elderly. We so easily forget about them. Mary MacGregor, a public health nurse, came to talk to the class before we visited the home and she told us that it is terrible how many children put their parents in one of these places and then rarely go to visit them. One of the most poignant sights in an old folks home is to see the memento's of the past life of the old person— yellowed clippings from the paper about their children's accomplishments, a granddaughter's hair ribbon, a tattered old picture of a young and happy family, medals, bits of nondescript relics of the past that bring back memories of happier times. And when their loved ones don't come to visit, their hearts ache.

As we left we stopped briefly in a room where two old ladies sat in silence. It was a sad sight. One of them had been burned and her face was disfigured. The other old lady apparently couldn't speak. But the students waved and said hello as they passed by and the nurse said that even though the ladies did not acknowledge them, they were probably thrilled at being greeted by them.

In our discussion class the day after our visit to the home one of the students expressed her concern that so many of the elderly had no one to visit them. She told us that in her neighborhood there were Japanese people who have the grandparents living with them. The student remarked at how well the Japanese take care of their old people. "They would never think of putting them in a rest home," she said. Another student spoke up and said that in the "old countries" of Scandinavia the elderly are always taken care of by the children and grandchildren. We discussed why we in this country are so unwilling in general to have old people living with us? The problem is a complex one and many ideas came out of the discussion. The general consensus was that, in spite of certain inconveniences, elderly parents should preferably be cared for at home with one of their children.

In this regard I cut out a column from *Dear Abby*[1] and read it to the class:

Dear Abby:

About seven years ago you printed a letter in your column signed "TOO LATE."

Abby, I must have read that letter a hundred times. I finally cut it out and framed it because I realized that I had been guilty of neglecting my own parents in their declining years. I made up my mind then and there that I would turn over a new leaf while there was still time, and I did.

Not only did I try to make up for the times I was "too busy" to go to see them but I explained to my children how important it was to give their grandparents the pleasure of seeing them often. Now I know that I never will have to write a letter like the one I framed. Perhaps if you were to print that letter again, it would do for others what it did for me. God bless you.

GRATEFUL

Dear Grateful:

Thank you for your letter. Curiously enough the custodian of a cemetery wrote to tell me that "TOO LATE'S" letter had been framed and was hanging in the chapel. What a pity that it would be read by those for whom it was also too late. How much more good

89

might be accomplished were it posted on the bulletin board in a high school. Here it is:

Dear Abby:

I am the most heartbroken person on earth. I always found time to go everywhere else but to see my old gray-haired parents. They sat at home alone, loving me just the same. It is too late now to give them those few hours of happiness I was too selfish and too busy to give, and now when I go to visit their graves and look at the green grass above them, I wonder if God ever will forgive me for the heartaches I must have caused them. I pray that you will print this, Abby, to tell those who still have their parents to visit them and show their love and respect while there is still time. For it is later than you think.

Life! When a person is sparked with an enthusiasm for life, there is hardly a more beautiful sight. Just last week a girl whom I had in class, and has since graduated, came back and burst in excitely to tell me of a place we could go for our field trips in Religion class. "I've been working at a nursing home all summer and I just love those old people. They're neat. If the students here could only see how much fun these old people are they would want to work there too. What they need is love and it's so easy just to stop and talk to them for a little while, to listen to them tell of how it was when they were young—all the things that are important to them. This is what they need and they give you so much in return, more understanding and patience, a sense of history, insights into human nature, so many things that can help you grow."

We had some marvelous discussions and gained valuable insights into human nature from this unit: The Teenager and the Aged. I scribbled down a note to myself as I heard the students discussing the problems and opportunities we have as Christians with regard to the elderly.

"These kids astound me. They're deep thinkers if you give them half a chance. Please keep thinking! Please keep discussing! Please keep *listening* to each other! Circumstances of life are as many and varied as leaves on the ground in autumn, but basic values give form and meaning to our lives. Christian values of love, respect, honor, and concern should be the driving force of our lives."

At the nursing home we visited the lady in charge told us of how the people there looked forward to death, how death was not looked upon as something terrible and horrendous, but rather as a relief, a change to a new and younger life free of the burdens of old age.

This struck the thirty one members of my Pepsi

"BE-ATTITUDES"

Generation hard. One wrote:

"At my young age I don't even think about death.
I am afraid that I would die unprepared and that I
would die in moral sin.

"When I get old and feeble I hope that someone
would care enough about me to help. I have two
grandparents left and I seem too selfish even to go see
them or even call them up. I don't think that I am
practicing my Christianity very well because I am not
concerned with others. But someday I'll be sorry when
my grandparents die."

Another said:

"The problems of old people are something I never
really thought of much. I have only been to one
nursing home in my life and this one was quite modern
and, at the time, I couldn't see anyone in bed. There
were people in wheelchairs but everyone seemed happy.
When we went to the nursing home last week my eyes
were really opened. I knew that the old suffered but
I never saw the suffering until I saw those people last
week. I tried to look for the 'person' inside those old
bodies and for many it was hard to see but when I
looked hard enough I could see that someone was really
there.

"As for death, I know a lot of old people are looking forward to it. I think they're very lucky to know that
they are going to die because this way they can be
more spiritually prepared. In the nursing home I
mentioned before, we were visiting my great aunt and
uncle. My great aunt had a dress that she only wore

on very special occasions. She took it out and showed my mom and beamed just like a child and said, 'This is the dress I'll be layed to rest in.' At the time it was difficult for me to understand how people could look forward to death. I think one reason why it was so hard for me was because my father died last summer and to me death was the worst thing that could happen. But now I can see that the dead are probably a lot better off than we are now. They have attained their goal. If anything, I think we should be almost envious of them. They're with God and happy and we're here and we still have our problems before us. I know now that I can look forward to it. I only hope I'm really ready when it comes."

Yes, death is not easy to face, but I feel we must face it during life, try to examine it from all sides, because in doing so we face reality, and that's the only way to live. Nothing is as certain as death! If we live life as Jesus intended us to, we will be best prepared for death.

Students often have an insight into life that we don't credit them with:

"One lady in particular seemed especially happy. She was walking all around in the room talking to everyone, showing off her new bathrobe. I did notice that almost all of the women have ribbons in their hair, probably to cheer everyone up and to brighten up the women themselves. All ribbons seem gay and even when you're in the worst of moods it adds to your appearance and makes you look somewhat happy on the outside even though you may feel lousy.

"When we walked into one room, an old lady took me by the hand and kept saying over and over again, 'Will you help?' I felt really sorry for her. One of the nurses said that that's all the lady ever says, 'Will you help me?' She reminded me of the many old people who are put into nursing homes and forgotten about. They rarely see the outside world again except through the window frame and even then its just a small section and not very realistic of what things are really like."

Each person is unique. To highlight this I would like to quote the reaction to our outing on the part of two different girls in the same class. Here is what they wrote:

"Well, the truth is that when it came to this topic, my interest was totally gone. For some reason I hadn't the slightest concern about discussing the old. Maybe it was because I don't, or didn't, think of it as much of a problem. Maybe I thought there were worse things going on that we should discuss instead of something 'not so drastic' or is it? That's what I tried to ask myself, and also I

"Age makes for good flavor!
Old people are:
Homemade bread,
Homemade cookies,
Hand-knit mittens,
And old wood stove
On a snowy night,
Crocheted pillow slips
And baby clothes,
Rag dolls and
Whistling teapots,
False teeth and
Roll-down wall beds,
Model T Fords,

asked myself, 'Why aren't I concerned?' I think I've figured out that the reason for not being concerned is that I've never been related with the problem of my grandparents. My dad's parents are still living and married. They are in their sixties, but are fairly young in body (pretty active). My mother's dad (her mother's deceased) is retired but living in a nice apartment, has a car, and gets around a lot. He is a nuisance once in a while when he starts talking about all his girl friends and going out to the Elks Club, where most of his time is spent. Other than that, I haven't experienced anything much more (I'm fortunate), although I am aware of the problems that others do have, and the problems of whether to place them in a rest home. And I have to admit, too, that I am undecided as to whether these rest homes are 'good' for them or not.

Pipes and old lavender,
Everything wonderful
But just about gone.
Old people, to me, are the most wonderful people in the world. They are as unique, lovable, and varied in personality as tiny children. Yet they are adults, people of a different age, a different world, living history books with that precious homey 'just like Grandma used to make' touch. We can know about the things of today, and the people, but so much of yesterday was never written down, so we have to know and love these people before they leave. If we don't there's just too much we'll have missed, and in our time of speed, we can't afford to not slow down. Old people are people, and they're neat!"

"BE-ATTITUDES"

In cases it is, in cases it isn't. It does depend a great deal on the motive of the children. I know some children do put their parents in a rest home in order to get them 'out of their hair.' It's sad, and I've found out it is a problem."

Yes, old people are people and they're neat!

Finally, one boy wrote the following which pretty well summarizes our unit on the Christian Teenager and the Aged:

"I knew an old man once. He was in his sixties I guess. He was crippled and he drank quite a bit. I remember going over to his house (he was a neighbor) and visiting him every single day because his wife worked during the day. This was about five or six years ago but I'll never forget how grateful he was to see me. Not that I was something special; it was just that he had someone to talk to. I didn't realize then how lonely he must have been. In fact I remember him offering to pay me something like $2.00 a *week* just to visit him and at that time $2.00 was a fortune to me. I don't think I truly understood until now that I really think about it.

"This is what old age is all about. The book and everything we talked about in class is rolled up into this man who has died. His manners were poor. He was

96

sloppy. He did no work. All he did was sit around. He wasn't very bright and yet I never noticed that in all the time I knew him. I just thought he was a nice man."

1. Reprinted with permission.

The Everyday World

DID YOU EVER have anyone step up to you and say, "Good Afternoon! Are you a Christian?" Would it throw you if somebody did? This is exactly what our class did one week in our pursuit of what it means to be a Christian in real, practical everyday life.

I have felt for a long time that Catholicism and Christianity should be more a part of our practical everyday life or else it is not genuine. I suggested one day in class that we go to the Boeing Airplane Company and just walk around and see if being a Christian meant anything to the people working there.

As I looked out over the class I saw a hand raised in the back of the room and, when I acknowledged the boy, he asked, "What's Boeing got to do with being a Christian?"

"That," I said, "is precisely the question we want to answer, because the Boeing Airplane Co. is the

center of the lives of about 30,000 people in the
Seattle area who work there and many thousands
more who are indirectly affected by the company.
Many of you will be working for Boeing. If our
religion cannot carry over into our jobs then it's not
much of a religion. It becomes a Sunday-go-to-meet-
ing exercise, a show, a social gathering with tea and
fancy cookies. But our religion, if it is to be a way
of life, has *got* to mean more than Sunday-go-to-
Mass time."

When I called the Personnel Department of the
Renton Plant and told the supervisor what I had in
mind he was a little bewildered at the request, but
nevertheless was cooperative and very hospitable.

I think he asked me twice on the phone, "Did you
saw this was a *Religion* class?" "Yes," I said, "We'd
like to see Boeing's operations, watch the people and
see if our Christian religion can be a practical way of
life while working at Boeing." Well, it was OK with
him. He must have felt like the gangly kid in the
back of the class who asked, "What's Boeing got to
do with being a Christian?"

We arrived at the Renton Plant where the Boeing
Company assembles the 737, 727 models and the
mock-up model of the Super 747.

The Supervisor met us at the gate and immediately gave us a whole handful of papers and "P.R."

brochures telling what Boeing does, and the philosophy of its existence.

Despite the fact that Boeing is a mega-company,
and might lose the individual in a series of numbers,
I think its philosophy is Christian. A chart explaining
this philosophy, comparing our system of government
with Communism, Socialism and Fascism, from an
economic point of view and considering at all times
individual personal worth, would look like this:

ECONOMIC FACTORS:	OWNERSHIP OF THE TOOLS OF PRODUCTION	COMPETITION	LABOR
COMMUNISM	The state should own all the tools of production.	Prohibits it and enforces State-cooperation and State planning by police action.	Amount and kind of work ordinarily prescribed and compelled by the State.
SOCIALISM	The state should own basic industries such as power, coal, steel, etc.	Prohibits it, constructs a national plan. Can compel compliance with plan even in privately-owned industries.	Legal compulsion is used when non-monetary appeals fail: i.e., security, patriotism, public acclaim, power, joy of public service, etc.
FASCISM	Private ownership which is solely a privilege granted by the State.	Subscribes to it but largely eliminates it through State-fixing of prices and production quotas.	Worker-management syndicates for planning production under State controls. Freedom clearly a privilege granted by the State.
OUR SYSTEM	Individual ownership of property under constitutional guarantees of certain inalienable rights.	Competition as an inherent right established by custom and upheld by law. Determines efficiency, technological progress, price and standard of living.	Complete freedom of choice concerning place and kind of work.

MANAGEMENT	GOVERNMENT'S RELATION TO BUSINESS	BUSINESS ETHICS
Party membership required of managers. Authority backed by police action.	Government should own and operate all economic units. State ownership to be achieved by revolution and maintained by a "dictatorship of the proletariat."	State laws, administrative regulations, and party edicts become the standard of conduct (in the absence of moral standards).
Stress laid on non-monetary incentives. State compulsion implied in the execution of state plans.	Government should own and operate all basic industries. State should achieve this gradually by constitutional means.	Reliance is placed on voluntary codes of good business practice, but State control tends to force them into the realm of legal compulsion for the realization of a State goal.
Management-worker syndicates plan and carry out State plans. State compulsion in carrying out State plans is implied.	Government should supervise and operate a State-constructed master economic plan, compelling such obedience as is necessary.	All ethical codes tend to reflect the predominant myth of State omnipotence. Party edicts achieve the status of legal compulsion through the avenue of police action.
Management is dependent upon voluntary acceptance by customers, employees and owners.	Government's broad function is fostering individual freedom for initiative and productivity. It's restrictive function is one of prohibiting those acts that would injure the individual or curtail freedom.	Religious concepts of divine origin of man from the Jewish-Christian heritage provide moral principles underlying the codes of business ethics.

On the tour we walked through a building that must have had the floor space of six football fields. The entire area was filled with men at drafting tables. Men dressed in .wash 'n wear short sleeve dacron shirts, thin ties, dark trousers, and winged-tip shoes. Each was working on some separate part of the huge 747 plane. The guide told us that when a young man enters engineering school he has grand ideas of designing a new revolutionary plane, and in reality he ends up designing a nut that will fasten a chair more securely to the floor of a plane.

Then we went to two gigantic assembly plants, one where thousands of men and women scrambled over silver airplanes each doing a little job, from riveting wings to attaching electrical cables for light switches. It was an impressive sight to see.

This is an age of pragmatism. If a thing works, it's good. Making airplanes is practical. They work. How about practicing Christianity? Does that work? When we got back into the classroom the next day the students had varying reactions. One of the common observations was the impersonality of the huge plant, people walking past each other like parts passing on an assembly line. The place seemed devoid of smiles.

The question was, "How do you love your neighbor as yourself in such an environment?" One student saw "doing an honest day's work where it would be easy not to," as a "Christian way" to exist at Boeing. Another said, "As I toured Boeing and evaluated the work that was being done I didn't give much thought to whether Christianity was relevant at Boeing. I couldn't really see where it was. Then I started thinking about my moral obligations and came to the conclusion that Boeing provides jobs for thousands of people. The policy of the company is *not* to discriminate. They hire people of all races, colors and creeds. Every business has a moral obligation to do this. Boeing does. Boeing also provides a means of transportation and communication by the great airplanes it makes. During the war Boeing made airplanes that helped keep America strong and independent. They are now trying to perfect a device for moon landings. You might not think there is Christianity at Boeing, but if you look around you'll find it."

If you look around . . . that's the big question today. We are so distracted by a million noises and sights, vexations to man's spirit. Television pours out inane programs that hypnotize viewers. Rock radio stations keep the teenager's mind scrambled.

We have to have time to consider life-values and be directed by them. We have to find time to pray. Psalm eight suggests that God has made us a little

105

5

less than the angels. Yet if you look around today some poor people live as if they were a little less than machines!

I suppose it is the American genius to strive for the practical and pragmatic, and one day the thought hit me, "Why not have the students go out and interview the man in the street to find out exactly what he thinks about his Christian religion?" So on Day One we spent the entire class period considering what to do, and decided on the following:

Our purpose was to ask people point-blank if they considered themselves Christian, why they thought they were, and how their Christianity influenced the way they lived.

Secondly, we filled an entire blackboard with places in the city where we were to go—to the shipyard, a posh women's store, a dime store, a police station, a hospital, the hippie district at the University of Washington, and the streets of the city of Seattle.

Here is the form used in asking people about their commitment to Christ as Christians:

In our search for Christianity and Christ in the city I would like to give you a few guidelines:

#1. BE COURTEOUS AND POLITE AT ALL TIMES.
#2. BE CONFIDENT. BE PLEASANT. SMILE.

*(Be assured that
the people you
interview will be
impressed by you
if you respect them.)*

Here are a few questions that might serve as a guide
or help in interviewing:

1. My name is .... I am a senior
   at Blanchet High School. As a project for our
   Religion class we are trying to find Christians and
   Christ in Seattle. Would you mind if I asked you
   a few questions?

   1. Are you a Christian?
   2. Some people today are saying Christians go
      to Church on Sunday only and cease to be
      Christians during the rest of the week (Sunday
      Christians). How do you feel about this?
   3. Do you think Christians, as Christians, can
      help in solving some of our Nation's problems:
      Civil Rights, War, Loosening of Morals, etc.
   4. Do you think Christians are too passive (won't
      take a stand for what they believe, follow the
      crowd like sheep, etc.)?
   5. Some say that teenagers today are pagans with
      no religious convictions. How do you feel about
      this?

6. (Feel free to use any or none of these questions. If you wish to ask your own, great!) (Be sure to write things down, or else you'll forget.)

Remember the distinguishing marks of a Christian:

1. Feed hungry   Love Your
2. Give drink to thirsty   Neighbor
3. Clothe naked   As Yourself.
4. Shelter homeless   Love the Lord
5. Take care of poor   Your God
6. Help handicapped   with your whole heart,
7. Visit imprisoned   mind, soul and strength.
8. Worship God

(Mt 25)

At first, the students were a little hesitant, shy perhaps about going out and asking these people questions. I suppose it is another American trait that we leave people alone. Let them do their own thing, as it were, no matter what it is. This, of course, leads to the indifferentism of the large city where people pass one another on the street as if they didn't exist. This happens in any big city.

There's something about teenagers that is attractive and when they stepped up to the "man in the street," introduced themselves politely and said, "Are you a Christian?" the interview was captured. For example, two girls stopped a tough construction worker and put some of the questions to him: "Are you a Christian? How do feel about Sunday Christians? Do you feel you do your job as a Christian?" etc. This rough-bearded, pot-bellied Hardhat was very kind to the kids, and told them he was a Christian, but that he didn't think he did his job *as* a Christian. He thought "Christians should be more aware of their religion in the way they live." He didn't think they were. He thought that if more people were not afraid to practice their religion the world would be a better place.

One interesting thought comes from this. Why is it that "religion" is something we put under wraps? Why are we afraid to admit openly by our actions that we are Christians? I think it is important to answer this question, because it gets to the heart of the matter of what religion is largely all about. Too often religion has the connotation of formalism, a frozen-faced humorless seriousness. "Religion" so conceived is bound to strike one as puritanical and unbending. It conjures up images of black clothes, folded hands, and quiet speech, kneeling, standing and sitting with the least amount of movement possible. Perhaps this is why some people who otherwise tend to "lead a good life" and "live by the golden rule,"

109

don't see why it's necessary to go to church on Sunday. Their concept of religion is superficial and unreal.

One girl wrote in her paper:

> "When our assignment was given last week I was just a little frightened to go out and ask people if they were Christians. It seemed to be an embarrassing subject, because 'Christian' is a word most people don't use in everyday conversation. Perhaps this is where the problem lies. If Christianity is a way of living your life, as your life, as it should be, then it should be as commonplace in our daily life and language as what we're eating for supper."

That's the point. Jesus is the essence of Christianity. He's what it's all about. Christianity is a religion that has at its center the "I-Thou-We" relationship of life in Christ, as Father Haring says, and it must be as vital to us as breathing. Our young people are looking for this authentic Christ-life. They are seeking the real Jesus, someone with whom they can identify, a man of strength and compassion, a man of understanding, a man with a sense of humor, a man of passion, a man alive!

If religion is to be meaningful to them, it must be fully human as well as divine. God so loved the world that he sent his only Son to be our Savior. In coming to earth, Jesus became a man like us in all

110

things except sin. Because he was fully human, to be like him we must be fully human too. We must recognize the inherent worth of being human. And more, because our dignity as sons of God and coheirs with him of heaven requires that we *excel* at being his followers.

Teenagers feel a need for authentic Christian living today. They seem to me to be in a state of Christian weightlessness—they are easily moved from one position to another. Their faith means *something*, but a vague something. Here's what one student said:

> "I thought that our going out into the city to interview people was really a good idea, after we did it. I thought at first that people would not want to discuss their Christianity but I was wrong. The lady we talked to at John Doyle Bishop's was more than eager to answer our questions. And we found that once we started more questions came automatically. But at times I wondered if she really knew what we meant by 'Christian.' "

One of the modern phenomena of our day that continues to astonish me about Christians is the attitude people have toward Christ and religion. For example, I shiver to hear Christians use the name "Jesus" or "Christ" in swearing to give emphasis to what they say. Really, if one analyzes that mode of acting, it is frightening. Jesus for them doesn't really

111

exist. And if they go to Mass on Sunday it can only be out of social grace, because it is the "thing to do."

The name of Jesus rarely, if ever, comes up in conversation. Why not? If he is to be followed as the Incarnate Son of God, if his philosophy, or way of life is really that, a way of life, then to use his name only blasphemously is a contradiction in terms. Why can't we talk about Jesus? Why does the name of Christ stick in our throat in our ordinary conversation? Why do people get embarrassed and blush when the name of Jesus is included in an everyday, ordinary conversation?

Here are a couple of paragraphs from student papers after they stepped into the "real world" and asked, "Where's Christ?"

> "The past week we've done a lot of things but I think that the most interesting were the interviews that the kids brought back. We went out into the city and interviewed people on the street. In this way we hoped to get a cross section of Christian ideals or lack of them."

> "Our group went to the District and interviewed. It's a funny thing but for some reason hip people are very big believers in Christ. I'd say practically all of them believe and know a lot about Christ. I suppose they feel that they relate to him because he was a guy who was different and stood up against the world and

changed it. They don't seem to go in for psychedelic religion and stuff like that; and their oriental trends are Christian-oriented."

"All in all the interviews rather depressed me. Most of our interviews seemed to come out rather flat. I think about three of all that the class interviewed were proud and glad and truthful about saying what they thought. The rest of the answers seemed to be stereotyped Christianity or stereotyped shock treatments. This proves that we have got a long way to go toward our goal as Christians. If people aren't as glad to tell people what they feel about their God as much as they'd like to complain about their parking ticket then something is wrong."

Another student:

"There are many ways of being a Christian and many ways of defining one too. But the main point is how we are able to really carry out the true meaning into the everyday world of life."

"This doesn't stop at saying that a Christian is supposed to love his neighbor and do good things only. It's being really aware that people exist and have a purpose in life. I discovered this when we went to the U. District for our religion trip. There were all kinds of people walking the streets, all with a different purpose and aim in life."

"One of the first people we stopped to ask was a man who had just gotten out of his car to do some

113

shopping. When asked if he had a few minutes to answer a few questions for our survey, he was more than glad to answer them, but as soon as we said the world 'religion' he got real upset and walked away with the words, 'Don't bother me with religion. I don't have one.' This was so startling that I could hardly believe my ears. After that I finally realized that being a Christian doesn't just include going to Mass on Sundays and being good; it means doing what Christ did and wants us to do."

This face to face meeting of people with people, of the young with the old, and the young with the young is a tremendously valuable experience. When people can let down their defenses and find that Christ really does have a place in the modern world, its a wonderful and exciting revelation.

To really live like a Christian, relaxed, concerned, and confident, is the only way to live! But one has to *experience* what authentic Christian living is. It's a marvelous thing to see this in our youth. More than one talked like this:

"I thought that most of the people we'd ask would shove us off and go to seemingly more important duties. But surprisingly out of about twelve people we questioned only one told us to ask someone else because he was too busy. All but about two people said they were Christians. But none had thought of their work as being Christian until we brought up the relationship between work and religion. Only one person thought that she didn't have a rôle in society, and I

114

think this was because maybe she thought that her job was not vital to the company's success. When asked if a Christian could be a Christian just by going to Mass on Sunday, all of the people we talked to quickly stated that to be a Christian, one must be so *everyday* of the week. It didn't surpise me in the least when a rather middle-aged, tired looking Negro man we asked, answered back about living a true Christian life seven days out of every week, better worded than I've ever heard any answer before. I think his answer struck a note on the whole objective of this course: to be a Christian in the world; to link, tightly, the ways, means, and goals of religion and everyday life."

In class one day I went on and on about my theory that Christian people feel uneasy when you talk about Christ and Christianity to them in the marketplace. I continued that people are ashamed, will blush if another seriously brought the name of Jesus into a conversation at a cocktail party, or on the job. I said people don't have the slightest clue that their Christian way of life should be as comfortable to them in the store, or on the street or even in a bar, as it is in church. "In fact," I said, "I'll bet you that if you drop the name of Jesus in a conversation, other than swearing, either you will blush, or the person you are talking to will cough, clear his or her throat, look at the floor and be thoroughly embarrassed.

The next day we were to go to King County Hospital in Seattle, and the administrator told us he would show us how the hospital works, who worked there, what kind of patients were treated, etc. I suggested that somewhere along the line one of the students stop a nurse, doctor, kitchen employee, administration or office worker and say to them: "I think this is a fine Christian work you're doing taking care of the poor and sick like this." I bet the students, if they would have the courage to do it, that the person they stopped and spoke to would cough, shuffle his or her feet, blush, look at the floor and mutter some non-descript comment.

One of the students took me up on it! We had toured the entire hospital with a young man from the University of Minnesota who was doing his hospital administrator's internship at King County Hospital.

On the way out of the building she stopped him, looked him straight in the eye, and said: "I think this is a fine Christian work you are doing here." And he said, looking her straight in the eye, *without* shuffling his feet, or coughing or blushing: "Thank you very much. I enjoy the work."

My theory was shot down. Maybe people aren't really ashamed to admit they're Christians in the everyday world, off stage, as it were. Maybe Catholic-Christianity is more than just Mass on Sunday? Can Christ and Christianity be practical? What do you think?

The Environment

IN THIS CHAPTER I would like to present some of my ideas about culture and conditions that influence the teenager of today. We are creatures of our culture and environment, and our religious life will in large measure be determined by these two factors.

We live in a complicated world today. There are many reasons for this complexity, ranging from air pollution to communications. We live in the *instant* now. Today when one turns on a radio he gets instant sound. When he sits down to eat, he eats "Instant Breakfast." There is instant news reporting, not only in the city, but around the world by satellite hook-up. There is practically instant travel and mobility in high powered cars and jet planes and rockets.

It would be the understatement of the century to say that life today is more complicated than it ever was. Just one generation back life was not exactly primitive but it was a lot less chaotic. We didn't have cars then. The airplane was a fantastic dream. Space travel was science fiction. It took two weeks for a letter to travel from New York to San Francisco. Television was a fairy tale, and radios squawked and sputtered for a long time when you turned them on. We were hardly the "Global Village" that Marshall McLuhan says we are today.

Religious education and training, like art, reflects the age, culture and environment. The Baltimore Catechism is a perfect example of the relative simplicity of only a generation ago. Questions and answers were the format of religious education. If you had any question about God, self, others or religion, you only needed to go to the Catechism to look up the answer. Someone had thought up all the questions and had given all the answers. And who was to gainsay them? We lived in a much more neatly packaged world then.

Today it's a different story. All one need do today is to turn on the TV and within a few minutes get opinions, facts and presumptions from all over the world. News programs present live simultaneous broadcasts of experts in every field from all over the world every day. And when one is confronted with the opinions of reasonable men he is hard pressed at times to make a single, dogmatic judgment. The average viewer can absorb more information by watching television in one evening than our great grandparents could by reading books by kerosene lantern all night long.

When a teenager today is confronted with such a massive display of information and mis-information he must be confused. A teenager is physically emotionally and psychologically undergoing rapid and profound changes. And his world is changing too. To expect him to unquestioningly accept one simple answer to almost any question in any field today is unrealistic.

While studying the Bible in class I concentrated on different themes such as love, war, peace, children, changes of the seasons, etc. I asked the students if they knew of any themes like those in the Bible that were being sung about in the pop world of music. Well, I faced a forest of hands! And that began a long project of comparing the same themes with those that Bob Dylan, Simon and Garfunkel, John Lennon, Country Joe and the Fish, etc., are writing and singing about. What's the difference between the Bible's expressions of human life as it is really lived, and the musical expression of it today as it is really lived? The major difference lies, of course, in the fact that in the Bible, *God* is actively present and totally submerged in the affairs of man's life whereas he is all

119

too often absent in our cultures today. I think that it is imperative that we get our children to see him once again in our human condition.

We have not been doing this very effectively in the recent past. For example, I asked my Senior class of boys and girls, the vast majority of whom were products of Catholic homes and twelve years of Catholic schools these two questions: (1) What does being a Catholic mean to you? (2) What does the person of Christ mean to you? Here are some of the unexpected answers that I got:

> "To tell the truth, being a Catholic doesn't really mean a heck of a lot to me. What is it supposed to mean? Going to Mass and Communion every week, confession once a month, and putting your two-bits in the collection basket? Right now Catholicism holds little attraction for me because the ceremonies and such seem very shallow. I haven't been to confession in over a year and do not feel the need to. It just has no meaning to me. I go to Mass every Sunday, however probably out of force of habit and the 'threat' of sin. This isn't as hypocritical as it sounds because sometimes, I'll admit, I do get something out of the Mass. I guess I am a Catholic in name only, unable to leave the Church because of what my family and relatives would say. Maybe I'm just going through a rebellious stage and will have a change in my attitude as time goes on.

> "In spite of all this, however, I do not consider myself religionless. I am a Christian, or would like to

120

be, in the full sense of the word. Christianity, as I see it, is people, and people after all, are what it's all about. To love everyone, and treat them as your equals is the essence of Christianity. It's difficult to reach this stage, because as a human I can be snobbish, or cutting, etc. But I have set this as my goal and hope someday to overcome my weaknesses."

Another student:

"Being a Catholic doesn't mean a lot to me. I would prefer to think of myself as a Christian; not where Christianity is a set of beliefs, but Christianity as a way of life. To me being a Catholic means that a person has a certain set of beliefs (which I may or may not have), which sets him apart from the rest of the Christian world, and, ideally (though often far from true) a philosophy of love which is (or should be) the power that fosters him to that whole Christian world and makes him (me) one with it. The reason I took this class is because I don't see the philosophy of love practiced enough in 20th century U.S.A. In other words, being a Catholic is most important to me because it designates me as a Christian.

"The person of Jesus Christ as a god sometimes (most of the time) leaves me unmoved. I have, however, a great respect and admiration for the man. He was a man who fully practiced what he taught, that is, love. I don't always agree with all the trivial particulars that his followers credit him as desiring, but his main message, love of neighbor, is a message which all people pay attention to."

One girl honestly admitted:

> "To me, being a Catholic doesn't mean much except obeying the rules of the Church. What is more important to me is being a Christian. I'm probably just arguing words, but Catholic doesn't seem to include everything that Christian does. Catholic means being Christian, but Christian doesn't mean being Catholic to me. I don't especially like being a Catholic, but the Catholic Church includes most of my ideas and morals more than any other Church would. If I have to be in a Church, then it will be Catholic.
>
> "The person Jesus Christ is an ultimate goal to me. He is what I would class as the perfect ideal. I, myself, have no ambition to be this perfect, simply because it would take too much effort and after this perfection is reached, there doesn't seem to be anything left to look towards. It would be wonderful to put what he did into each day, but it would take more effort than I would care to use. This is what I feel at the moment. By tomorrow, I may have changed, depending on the mood I'm in."

It should be obvious from this that what our children understand about God, and what *we* think they understand are many times two different things. Here's another example:

> "To me being a Catholic means helping people all I can. I do not think that I should have to go to church every Sunday or go to confession. These things are really made up by the popes of past times; not

Christ. I think that to be Christian, one should help our friends and relatives and anyone we should come into contact with everyday of our lives. Some people will go to church every Sunday and receive Communion. The minute they get out of church they think they are so holy that they want nothing to do with anybody that needs help or sympathy. This is a phoniness that I cannot stand and I know of many of this type of Catholics."

"The person Jesus Christ, does not mean that much to me. I mean, I know who he is and what he has done for us, but I still I do not know nor can comprehend him as well as I would like to. I mean, you picture him up on some cloud, and I don't understand about heaven and hell. I think heaven and hell are just a state of mind."

I remember one teenager saying: "If parents with their maturity are confused today, just try to imagine what goes on in a teenager's mind when he is trying to decide on life values. Our lives are changing by the mere fact we're teenagers, but when we listen to the radio, watch television, read everything from *The New York Times'* 'Student Weekly' to the underground press, we are confused as to know who's right. There seem to be good arguments on both sides on everything from birth control to the arms race to violence in the streets. Who's to say who's right? We're confused."

And that is where you and I, that is where the

Church comes in. Confused they may well be, but I don't think this is bad. Confusion is another form of dynamics that can lead one to the truth. Confusion necessarily involves conflict of ideas and eventually, "Truth will out." In today's world the battle is too open, the spoils are too great to go into the great struggle for the salvation of mankind without confidence of one's purpose and plan.

As Jesus said in the Gospels: "If two kings are about to do battle, each sits down and calculates the strength of his army against the strength of his enemy. If he sees he is weaker he sends a delegation for peace. If he sees he is stronger he marches to meet the enemy." We can meet the forces of indifference, atheism and out and out evil, with strength and purpose. But there is a big *IF*. If we are truly *Christian*—that is to say, if we have Christ's mind and heart. He was a servant, a suffering servant. He was above all, kind and understanding. He was strong and "intolerant" of hypocrisy. He was fiercely opposed to man's indifference to God—think of his anger toward the money changers in the temple, and his description of "indifferent" people, calling them "vomit"! Jesus spoke of the cross. And no matter how you slice it the Calvary of suffering is inevitable, but in the end there is also the joy of resurrection.

We do teenagers a great disservice if we try to please them, if we try to bend to their wishes, if we

124

try "to make life easier for them, because-I-don't-want-you-to-have-it-as-difficult-as-I-did." Teenagers, or any one for that matter, thrive on an authentic struggle for an authentic goal. Nothing worthwhile getting is easy to obtain. It is to the eternal credit of President Kennedy that he sparked the youth of America to use their energy for good in the Peace Corps. And it is to the credit of America's youth that they are willing to live on as little as $2 a day, to risk illness in a foreign land, to live a life of service, and to suffer loneliness for the sake of our Country's ideals. Today, thanks to the recent renewed support of Congress, the Peace Corps is still vigorous and effective and growing. In terms of dollars and cents the costs are meager, but what the young people are doing for our Country's *soul* is incalculable.

They are turned on, and totally involved in today's society. Generally speaking they are realists, and are not seeking escape from the world or from "straight society." They're authentic. They're genuine.

There's a lot of talk about the generation gap today, a lot of talk about the credibility gap between the young and old. In the area of young people's religious convictions there's a growing credibility gap because of what they see in the generation gap. They're saying: "Don't tell me how to be a good Catholic. Show me." Credibility in the Catholic faith is best fostered by good example which is both genuine and sincere. Christ was an honest, genuine man. We must be the same. If we, as Christians, lead double lives of lip service to God and disservice to our fellow man we contribute to the dissolution of his kingdom.

The big worry about kids today is their relativism —"I will do what *I* think is right." "A man has to follow his own conscience." This is true, but Lee Harvey Oswald followed his conscience when he pulled the trigger and murdered our President. Judas followed his conscience when he betrayed his Master. Where does relativity stop and dogmatism begin? There is no easy answer. Jesus was a man who told us to love. Love is relative. There are degrees of intensity, and different subjects and objects. Love often deals with greys, not blacks and whites. But true love also draws the line. There's no selfishness in it. There was selfishness in Judas's kiss and Oswald's hand. There is selfishness in driving a car stoned on marijuana— or liquor. There is selfishness in *using* another.

Jesus wasn't a situationist. He was quite dogmatic, but at the same time he was very understanding. He listened. He tried to understand. He didn't judge people: "Will no one condemn you? Neither will I. Go and sin no more."

There is a lot of talk about change now, but today's younger generation wants to change the talk to action. Those of us who have the responsibility to guide young people in the development of their life-attitudes must realize that we will waste the best years of our lives perpetuating the status quo, if we don't "get with it." If we don't try to be totally alive to the "now," totally living now with the hope of a future life. The pursuit of truth is never static. It is ever on-going, ever uplifting, ever discovering.

We as adults have an obligation to lead young people to a realization of their potentiality, their goodness, their capacity for love and giving. We must encourage in them a sense of wonder and, if it is not already there, we must plant it. We must try to help them see God is the totally Other; the mysterious, dynamic person-love-force that guides this world and universe and each single person with a wonder-full order. We must seek God, like a child playing hide-and-seek with his father. The father knows the child is looking and always sees the child and will eventually show himself to the child with hugs and embraces and joyful laughter. And in our pursuit of God we must seek to *experience* God totally with all our being—body, soul, emotions, fears, joys, pleasures, pains —totally! So in "teaching" children or teenagers, or adults, for that matter, about God we must lead them to *experience* God's presence in their own lives by our example. We can't know God and love him purely intellectually. This denies the basic nature of man.

"BE-ATTITUDES"

This is well illustrated by the following story.

"One summer night in a seaside cottage, a small boy felt himself lifted from bed. Dazed with sleep, he heard his mother murmur about the lateness of the hour, heard his father laugh. Then he was borne in his father's arms, with the swiftness of a dream, down the porch steps, out onto the beach.

"Overhead the sky blazed with stars. 'Watch!' his father said. And incredibly, as he spoke, one of the stars moved. In a streak of golden fire, it flashed across the astonished heavens. And before the wonder of this could fade, another star leaped from its place, and then another, plunged toward the restless sea. 'What is it?' the child whispered. 'Shooting stars,' his father said. 'They come every year on certain nights in August. I thought you'd like to see the show.'

"That was all: just an unexpected glimpse of something haunting and mysterious and beautiful. But, back in bed, the child stared for a long time into the dark, rapt with the knowledge that all around the quiet house the night was full of the silent music of the falling stars.

Decades have passed, but I remember that night still, because I was the fortunate seven-year-old whose father believed that a new experience was more important for a small boy than an unbroken night's sleep. No doubt in my chidhood I had the usual quota of playthings, but these are forgotten now. What I remember is the night the stars fell, the day we rode in a caboose, the time we tried to skin the alligator, the telegraph we made that really worked. I remember the 'trophy table' in the hall where we children were

128

encouraged to exhibit things we had found—snake skins, seashells, flowers, arrowheads, anything unusual or beautiful.

"I remember the books left by my bed that pushed back my horizons and sometimes actually changed my life. Once my father gave me *Zuleika Dobson,* Max Beerbohm's classic story of undergraduate life at Oxford. I liked it, and told him so. 'Why don't you think about going there yourself?' he said casually. A few years later, with luck and a scholarship, I did.

"My father had, to a marvelous degree, the gift of opening doors for his children, of leading them into areas of splendid newness. This subtle art of adding dimensions to a child's world doesn't necessarily require a great deal of time. It simply involves doing things more often *with* our children instead of for them or to them."[1]

The pursuit of God is always an adventure, many times surprising, and many time exhilarating. It's not enough to *teach* children about God, we must *experience* him with them.

When we say, "I know God," we cease to really grasp him. God is the unknowable. He realized this, so to let us in on the awesomeness of the Trinity's life he became incarnate. Jesus is knowable. And since he is also the fullness of God's revelation to man, we can know something more of God than was ever heretofore possible. To know Jesus is to love. And,

129

in the words of St. Thomas More, the man for all seasons:

"It isn't finally, a matter of reason; finally it is a matter of love."

1. Excerpt from "The Night the Stars Fell," by Arthur Gordon, The Reader's Digest, October 1964. Copyright 1964 by The Reader's Digest Assn., Inc.